BLUM BO

Beach in the Bed and

COLLECTED POEMS AND ARTWORKS

VOLUME 4

June Mary Aviva Treister (née June Mary Scott) was born in Ipswich, Suffolk in 1927, daughter of Alice Joyce Lay and Basil Keeble Scott, grocer and provision merchant, whose father was headmaster of Wortham School. Although artistic she was unable to follow art as a career and entered the secretarial profession, first working in the Public Health Department of the East Suffolk County Council and afterwards the HQ of the Eastern Electricity Board. During WWII she was a member of the Girls Nautical Training Corps. In 1951 she moved to London taking a position as secretary to Maksymilian Treister who she later married, working with him as a company director in his electronics firm until their retirement in 2005. In 2013, after a gap of 70 years, she returned to art making. She has two children, a daughter Suzanne, an artist and a son Richard, a photographer. She lives in London.

Beach in the Bed and Crab in the Hat

COLLECTED POEMS AND ARTWORKS

VOLUME 4

JUNE TREISTER

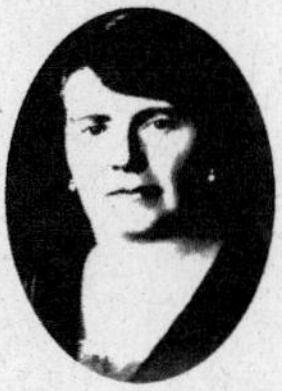

BLUM BOOKS

BLUM BOOKS

First published in Great Britain 2023

by Blum Books, 137 The Galleria, Pennack Road,
London SE15 6PW, England
email: blumbooks@blumbooks.com
www.blumbooks.com

Printed and bound in England

Designed and edited by Suzanne Treister

Cover image: *Crab in the Hat,* June Treister, 2021

All works reproduced in this volume were made by June Treister between 2020 and 2023

Acknowledgements
I would particularly like to thank John Tygier for his introduction, Adrian Dannatt for his essay and my daughter Suzanne for her time spent on designing and editing this book.

ISBN 978-0-9927822-3-8

To my cousins Juliette and Linda

CONTENTS

ILLUSTRATED ARTWORKS

Some Kind of Leaves
Hyacinths and Anemones
Mother's Day Flowers
Space Flowers
Space Flowers 1
Blue Space Flowers
Three Moons
Green Space Flowers
Square and Triangular Space Flowers
Circular Space Flowers
Space Candles
Space Candles 2
Space Village
Mountains
Space City
London Pavement with Tissue, Coffee Cup and Utility Hole Cover
London Pavement with Utility Hole Covers
Country Lane with Moss
London Pavement - Corner of Broadhurst Gardens
Pandemic
Country pavement with grass and snow
Palette Trouser Monoprints (A series of 12 works)
Dream Drawing: Bowl of Washing on a London Bus
Crab in the Hat
Beach in the Bed
Pink Polish Cup
June's Painting of Suzy's Tree of Life
Hanging Apple and Banana
Sewing Kit
Tomato
Granny Smith – An Apple
Bananas, Tomato and Cucumber
Strawberries for a Strawberry Gentleman
Bears 1
Father and Baby Bear
An Axat Bear 1
An Axat Bear 2
Arctic Scene, Polar Bear and Seal
Axat Bear 3
Granny Smith Apple
A wooden French Country Man
Granny Smith Apple with Pink Background
Robin

Tigers
Red Sails in the Sunset
A Red Apple
Red Tomato, Red Cherries and Raspberries
Space Bird with Worm
London Maps in Space
Yeats and Wordsworth
Yeats
Picnic at Rennes le Chateau
A History of My Car Number Plates + Accident
A History of My Car Number Plates 2
A History of My Car Number Plates
Hotels
A Pottery Dalmation Dog
Flowerpot in the Pyrenees
Play House Shed Hut
Polar Bear
English Pickles: Colmans, Ketchup, Branston
English Pickles: Branston
English Pickles: Colmans

Introduction

When I first read June's poems and saw her paintings it was like finding the missing pieces, her other other voice, her other view.

Through work and then marriage June joined the community of East European refugees, of émigrés as the French would have called them. Her Englishness made her somewhat exotic in her own country, while simultaneously absorbing another culture.

There is always a gentle precision to June's work, always a curiosity and openness, the type of person it would be a pleasure to be stuck in a lift with.

Her work moves from notes and glances to more formal pieces.

And there is the rarest of all qualities in her work, gentle wit.

June often seems entertained by the world around her in its grandeur and minutiae.

Her poems are full of people, observed, overheard and unjudged.

They are playful, sensitive, delighting in the everyday, amused, bemused and paradoxical.

The artwork varies in technique and style and provides a different but complimentary commentary.

There is a subtle continuity to the poems that links them one to another, as movements in a greater work.

John Tygier

TREES JET RUIN: JUNE TREISTER

There is nothing wrong with building a life around charity committees and home decoration and gardening and volunteering. Most beautiful, good things are done by women people scorn.

Gillian Flynn
Gone Girl

The poetics of normality is perhaps a particularly English paradox; this stretches from Chaucer's pilgrims through Jane Austen's domestic tribulations and the deadpan bleakness of Stevie Smith or Pinter to that recent hit TV series *Marriage* which made the extremely everyday, bordering the banal or boring, seems strange in its simplicity. This deliciously Anglo-Saxon genre, 'Brit Normcore' one might dare term it, can be as poignant as Barbara Pym, as comic as Mr Pooter in *Diary of a Nobody* or moody as Bill Nighy in the film *Living*. The hero is replaced by a bumbling anti-hero like Reginald Perrin or a detective like Miss Marple, not to mention such entirely ordinary and sad spymasters as George Smiley and Jackson Lamb.

June Treister is surely the new crowned Poet Laureate of such very-English-understatement, such poker-faced plain speaking. Treister's blankest of blank verse, as blank yet expressive as Buster Keaton's pale visage, can be extremely funny in its juxtaposition of the *ordinaire* and the *outré*, but also proves rich in *tristesse*, tinged with the ripe melancholy of North London, the blinking strip-lit anguish of our shopping aisles. As such it grants the pleasure of those conversations overheard on a suburban journey or at the bus stop itself, so determinedly ordinary, the comparative prices of items in different supermarkets, as to become almost Surreal.

For Treister's poetry is so resolutely matter-of-fact as to become almost avant-garde. As such it touches a very different genre, one might think of the nimble neo-doggerel of the late David Robilliard or the work of the celebrated contemporary Jewish poet Nachoem Wijnberg, who always boasts that a child of twelve could understand his poems. Wijnberg seeks clarity and validity, simplicity and straightforwardness, with a notable lack of metaphor. One might also cite the minimalist wording of Aram Saroyan (who actually entitled a work *At A Bus Stop*) or that recent book *Milk and Henny* by the young Brooklyn poet Peter BD. This does seem a notably North American writing-style, approximating the childish less for the sake of charm than stark statement. Here plain speech, demotic simplicity, is transmuted into a radical textual strategy, including a notable proto-feminist lineage that might stretch from Emily Dickinson though Gertrude Stein, Mina Loy and H.D. to Susan Howe and Harryette Mullen.

One should here acknowledge that whilst Treister Senior is very much the author of all these works they have been edited and refined, rearranged and reduced (like any fine stock) by her daughter Suzanne Treister. The latter, an award-winning multi-media artist, is all too aware of such avant-garde literary and conceptual gambits and could well claim a sort of co-authorship, a nice symmetry considering her mama's undoubted 'authorship' of herself! As such, this whole project might be read as a meta reverse-version of Sylvia Plath's letters to her mother, being actually emails the other way round, in this case from mother to daughter. Likewise, it could find comparison to the recent acclaimed memoir MOTHERs by the poet Rachel Zucker which incorporates actual email exchanges between herself and her intractable mama. But perhaps it would be most appropriate to consider Suzanne Treister's attention to her own mother's varied texts as a sort of high-level editorial mission comparable to Pound's work on the rough draft of Eliot's *Wasteland*.

It might also be appropriate to cite the promotion and veneration of the self-taught Cornish artist Alfred Wallace by his modernist admirers Ben Nicholson and Christopher Wood; having seen by chance the paintings of this Old Salt fisherman, working outside his cottage in St Ives, these avant-gardists devoted themselves to collecting, 'curating' and promoting his singular genius. The whole history of *soi-disant* 'Outsider' artists is inherently connected to those, *soi-disant* 'professional' practitioners who discover their work and are then able to bring them into the mainstream. But in this case nobody, least of all June Treister herself, nor her family, are claiming her as an 'Outsider' or 'Art Brut' artist. This is just an artist *tout court*, one of a certain age, who has finally returned to her practice to make what she makes.

However, there is an interesting parallel with the visual *oeuvre* of June Treister and that of her better known daughter, both of them encouraging and abetting the other. Considering June had not made art since adolescence and early adulthood she openly admits to being led back, lured, by the example of her celebrated offspring. Perhaps equally important was the practical inspiration of having art materials immediately to hand, there for the using. For one can sense Treister's renewed creativity when staying with her daughter and husband Richard Grayson (also a well-known artist) at their house in the Pyrenees; here she is provided with direct creative inspiration, the numerous 'Axat' studies, abundant time and limitless paper, canvas, coloured pencils and paint.

Mother and daughter artists, for obvious historical reasons, are less frequent than the traditional masculine equivalent of father-son or even father-daughter; one might think of Mary Newcomb and her daughter Tessa, Phyllida Barlow and Florence Peake, Jenny Holzer and Lili Holzer-Glier,

Betty Woodman and Francesca, Janet and Kathy Ruttenberg, Daphne and Emma McClure, Lizbeth Mitty and Dana James. There is an overt and strong female bond that operates throughout this dynamic, an essentialist feminist continuity in the place of any testosterone rivalry, a sense of mutual nurture. Such a lineage might well make a rewarding theme for a group exhibition, limning a matriarchal axis ambitious for domestic continuity and community, some shared creative homestead, rather than for surpassing individual achievement and recognition.

Whilst Team Treister clearly contains two very different artists, in every way, more recent work by June seems to be growing closer to her daughter's domain; this includes striking images of 'black holes' throbbing with otherworldly energy over varied zones, perhaps directly connected to Suzanne's own interest in such phenomena. June acknowledges her inspiration was a television programme on Black Holes that she just happened to see, a typically modest and honest explanation, but it could well be that the mother's taste for such strange attractors is some genetic penchant passed on to her daughter, an inherited curiosity for the galactic occult, rather than vice versa.

Yet even June's whirling Black Holes appear determinedly ordinary, paradoxically as 'down-to-earth' as cosmically elevated, lovingly rendered as a natural phenomena. And indeed they are so, for according to astrologers and physicists every 'Black Hole' is as real, actual, physical, as a loaf of Waitrose bread or the number 139 bus. The collector and patron Agnes Gund stated that 'art really does take you away from the ordinary' but how much more challenging to discover an art that does not seek transcendence or transformation but rather is anchored in a celebration of precisely that 'ordinary'. For Treister the spiritual and the ordinary are entirely intertwined, even her adoptive Judaism being described in terms of social events, tea parties, ice cream, a lunch with a synagogue speaker; but this prosaic, even keel would not necessarily exclude the eruption of Kabbalistic coincidence or indeed the coming of the Messiah.

As in her poem on Blake, for Treister details are everything, very literally 'God is in the details' and whilst Blake finds the mystical in the everyday June determinedly, with deadpan humour, finds the *everyday* in the everyday; 'the exhibition cards annoyed me', 'there definitely were too many people', her experience of this Blake exhibition is one that we all know far too well but rarely dare express so openly. Treister's vision is rooted in the specifics of place and personality, just as her love for her Judaism, an extension of her long love for her late husband, is very specifically an *amour* for a certain place, North London, and a group of people, her like-minded parishioners in the Reform Synagogue.

And the reality is that this is *our* reality, on the whole; a practical and pragmatic view of the world in which attention to detail, the one-step-at-a-time living of life can lead to some final epiphany, however minor. To quote Donald Judd, not the first artist one might immediately associate with June's oeuvre, 'it is what it is.' Or indeed in Frank Stella's notable formulation, 'what you see is what you see.' But what we see here, and what is so heartening in Treister's emergence as a poet and artist is precisely how she has grown bolder, more febrile in both imagination and execution throughout these last four volumes of her gathered works.

From still lives of whatever was before her, flowers or breakfast croissant, initially rendered in slightly cautious watercolour, Treister's vision and ambition has steadily expanded outward; now we are rewarded with bears in the Alps, space flowers and science-fiction moons, interplanetary candles and cities, distant mountains and even an Arctic polar bear and seal. These confident explorations of a vaster, daring domain, are now boldly rendered in oil on canvas, and who knows, perhaps next in ceramic or sculpture. One can only await with anticipation the next development in Treister's continually ascendent creative trajectory. For if the sky was previously the limit, which she has now entirely surpassed, shot beyond, there seems nothing to stop Treister to boldly go where no artist, let alone North London nonagenarians, has gone before.

Adrian Dannatt

Note on the title;
'Trees Jet Ruin' is an anagram of 'June Treister', one of several I minted to try and explore, in perhaps a slightly Kabbalistic manner, the possible ramifications and hidden meanings of her name. Within these I found all sorts of possibilities and projections, juxtapositions, perhaps even subject matter for her own future work. Entree Jurist, Jetties Rerun, Reinsert Jute, Jeers Nuttier (a group of jeering madmen), Jester Rue Nit (a clown at Niort-Souche Airport know as NIT), Inert Jet User or even, like a royal command to a kneeling technician, "Rise Jet Tuner !"

POEMS

Moon Painting

No
I've worked the painting
Out in my mind
And studied the sky
This evening
Looking at the various colours
Of the sky
And finally the small moon
So almost on the way to starting
Will paint it from my bedroom window
On the small canvas
The large canvas
I will do some time later

William Blake

A brief report of the Blake exhibition
Don't think I can emphasize
Anything in particular
Mostly pale brown-grey and cream drawings
Of reclining figures and flying figures
Many biblical
Closely exhibited on the walls
There were a lot of poems
Surrounded by paintings and drawings
As well as old books
Containing Blake's hand-written poems
With drawings around them

The explanation cards annoyed me
Because they had been placed too low
It hurt the back of my neck
To strain forward to read them
At a height fit only for children

There were a few children there
Tagging along behind their parents
Who wanted a day of culture
There definitely were too many people
We thought the gallery staff
Should have let people
Queue and stagger the entries

Free Black Cab

The 139 bus was on diversion
And I got out at the back of Waitrose
Forgetting that I should have stayed
While they drove down Canfield
And stopped at Priory Road
But that would have been a long way for me
To carry the beef

So I walked up to the side of Waitrose
And took a black cab
When I offered the fare of five pounds
The driver said
I don't want your money
It will give me a pleasure not to take the fare
I tried to persuade him
That I wanted to pay
but he insisted
I said thank you
And then followed a little discussion
When I told him I was 92

He was a real Londoner
Whose parents had split up
And his father had gone to live in a house on the Norfolk broads
Where he sits fishing every day

Enchanted Computer

The Song: 'Strangely Strange But Oddly Normal'

I can't make this play
Can you?
What is it all about?

I have heard it
On my computer tonight
As it suddenly appeared

A miracle!

Yes
That I heard it?
John Tygier replied to my email
An enchanted computer thing
Have a good day
Some sunshine and
Dry cold weather at last
Good for a walk

Not Fazed

I just said to myself
That I am not 'fazed'
By having to delete
Umpteen trash email messages
Which are a terrible nuisance
And wondered if I had spelt it right
My eyes have not allowed me
To find it in the dictionary
So could you tell me
If I am right or wrong please

Inside Out

Have you ever thought
That when taking an item of clothing off
When you say it's inside out
It's actually outside in

Synagogue Speaker

The lunch was at 12.30
But I missed that
having had a hospital appointment

The speaker was in full flow
At 1.25 when I walked in
And vehemently waived her arms up and down
Indicating me to sit down !!
I quickly sat down
At the nearest empty chair

Dying for a cup of tea
But the cups and teapot
Were on the other side of the table
And no-one took any notice of me
All eyes were on the well-known speaker
Who rushed off at 2.15
To an important meeting
Most people left
But I went to the table
And took a dish of fresh fruit

The lady who thanked the speaker
Had mentioned that the ice cream
Had been made by the speaker
I saw the box of ice cream
With a little left in it
And took it over to the table
Intending to have a spoonful
With my fruit

Whilst I was struggling
To open the square plastic box
Elinor quickly reached over
And slid it across the table
Calling to Janet and said
Here is your ice cream
I sighed
But that was that

About to leave
I could not find my long distance glasses
Searched my bags
Went to the entrance hall

To see if they were on the sofa
Where I had sat earlier
Oh dear
No they weren't there
Returned to the dining place
And found them on the fruit and ice cream table
So relieved

One of the organisers were there
And persuaded me to have a slice of tarte au citron
We chatted
And then I left to go on to the nearby Churchill Hotel
For tea
It's so comfortable there
And has a truly international flavour

Crazy Radio

A few days ago
I put the radio on
Beside the sofa where I sit
In the sitting room
I walked to the kitchen
And when I came back
The sound was coming from the corner of the room
Under the Tiffany light

It seemed very spooky to me
I returned to the kitchen
And when I came back again
The sound was coming from behind the sofa
Under the window

I sat down to listen to the radio
Fnding it hard to believe my ears
By what was happning
Only when I held the radio to my ear
Could I hear the sound
Coming from it

So what do you think was the reason
For all this spookiness ????

Lo and behold
Yesterday a similar thing happened
In the kitchen
When the sound from the radio
By the far wall
Was coming out of the boiler
By the window

There must be a reason for this ???+?

What is my Name?

What is my name?

The various names which I call myself

When I am talking to myself out loud..........

June

June Mary

June Mary Treister

Mrs Treister

Mrs T

Junoosh

Junushenka

Silly B – I.e. silly bee ..

M'dear

Dearie

Dearie me

Dopey woman

Foolish woman

Hopeless woman.......

It seems that I don't find anything complimentary to say to myself ---- oh dearie me !

VE day

Plenty of special programmes on radio and TV today
I got up at 8 o'clock today
A very good start for me
I am about to phone Juliette
I’ll wear my blue dress and shoes today

Corona 19 Virus 2020

Sitting on my
walking stick chair
supporting myself
on the lamp post at
the crossroads a
lady cyclist sped by
and sang
'holding on a lamp
post at the corner
of the street
watching the boys
go by'

I laughed – a minute
later the red mail
van slowed down
and the driver
called
Are you all right
miss?

A jogger crossed
over the road and
asked me if was ok
and then a
pedestrian asked if I
needed any help – I
was only sunning
myself in the street
in these days of
self isolation

People are so kind......................

when I came home

I saw four beautiful red roses in full bloom in the garden

Petrified

Suzy's friend Petra
From Hamburg
Came to stay with Suzy
Petra was siitting
On the balcony
Drinking
A cup of coffee
A spacecraft landed
On Parliament Hill Fields
Petra was ....
“petrafied”
And felt as if
Her brain was fried

Telephone Poem

One of my three telephone receivers
Fell out of my dressing gown pocket
Into the lavatory
I fished it out
Rinsed it
Dried it
And put it into a bowl of rice
For 48 hours
Not a pip came out
So I returned it to the rice
For another 48 hours
It pipped
Which prompted me
To put it on charge
After several days
It was evident
That it wasn't going to work again
So it's now in the bin

With only two receivers
To live on
I am constantly moving them around
And some of the time
I can't find either of them
The worst thing that has happened
Is when I have mislaid
Both of them

Yesterday one of them
Started bleeping loudly
At the same time
As the cooker failed to switch on

I pushed up the offending switch
But it slipped down
Right away
So no chance to cook
Everything had to go into the microwave

The only way to reconnect the phone
I found by trial and error

Was to call the landline
From the mobile
One night of this was enough
But a second night of it
Unbearable

I phoned for an electrician
And was told it was probably caused
By my kettle

How strange is that
The cooker wasn't even switched on
At that point

Now my cooker grill
As well as the oven
Has failed to work
I finally must buy a new cooker
When the lockdown ends
But my family won't allow me
To go to John Lewis
In Brent Cross

I am really missing going shopping
All these weeks
But that's a small problem
Compared with many other peoples' problems

Every day I spend a lot of time
Looking for my telephone receivers
Disappearing in all the rooms
Nearly an hour was spent
Searching for the second one yesterday
Until it came to light
Under my napkin on the kitchen table

Tonight I roamed from room to room
Again in search of a receiver
Without success
And found it right in front of me
On the coffee table

A favourite wristwatch of mine
Disappeared too
And turned up
Wrapped around a bracelet
Of the same shade

Unfortunately
My eyesight is not very clear
So that doesn't help
Does it
But life goes on

There are two controllers
For the stairlift
And one has gone missing too
My eyes are constantly on the lookout for them

My clocks

I am a very time conscious person

In the kitchen
There is a clock on the wall
And one on the table in front of me
Where I usually eat
Because I can't see the one
On the wall
Unless I am close up to it

In the bathroom
One on the wall
With grey hands
Which I cannot see clearly
Why it wasn't made with black hands
I really don't know

In the sitting room
My grandfather's clock
From when he retired
Which I wind when I remember
It has a lovely chime
And was made in Germany
In 1914

There is a carriage clock
On the TV unit
From my parents' home
Which I fail to wind up
As the battery keeps slipping sideways
Because the door does not lock properly

On the coffee table
Where I sit
There is a small clock
Which I have painted gold

In the bedroom
There is a normal alarm clock
Beside the bed as well as a
Small clock with a light switch

To use in the night

In the office
There is only one clock
On the wall
Which is easy to read

In the toilet
There is a clock over the door
Which I can almost see from the toilet
If I squint
Because it is a size too small
John Lewis only had a larger one in stock
I would have been better off
With a size in between the two

Lastly
There is no clock
In the spare bedroom
Except if someone is very occasionally sleeping there
I would put one of my alarm clocks
Beside the bed
Amen

Squirrel

My bedroom windows
Are usually open
All day
And walking through the hall this afternoon
I heard a noise
Coming from the bedroom

When I went into the room
Disappearing across the furniture
And out of the window
Was the bushy tail of a squirrel

It had knocked over a small tin
Of biscuits
And managed to push off the lid
But had no time
To eat the rice crackers
Once I'd disturbed it

Running over the controller
The squirrel had switched on the TV
With its tiny feet
A football match
Was in full flow

Humour

Why did the one armed man cross the road?
To go to the second-hand shop.
What does a sheep dog's bra do for you?
He makes a point and rounds you up.
There was a third one but I can't remember what it was
have a nice day

Ovaltine

The squirrel woke me up
It had knocked over the Ovaltine
Which I had not drunk

Prince Philip's Funeral and Tea Party at Windsor Castle

Windsor Castle with unbroken blue sky it was
Sunshine
A large quadrangle with grass in the middle
And several platoons of military from various regiments
About four regiments chosen by the Duke
Including those with the black busbies
They're the Horse Guards aren't they
They all stood on the grass
And then they brought the pony trap in
Pulled by 2 large horses
On the seats were his cap and gloves and little pink thing with the sugar lumps
Then the they started the procession
They loaded the coffin onto the open land rover
They moved off and walking behind were the four children
Charles and Anne and Andy and Edward
Anne's husband was there, Harry, then behind that came
Oh I don't know I can't remember
No the women were standing along the side by a wall
They moved all around the quadrangle
Past the pony trap
And when it arrived the Queen and all the mourners went into an entrance
At the side of the chapel
And then the pall bearers, different pall bearers from another regiment
Slowly moved the coffin onto their shoulders
And slowly carried the coffin up the steps
There must have been at least 40 steps
Then they stood on the flat step
They received commands from a soldier when to move
While they were standing there
There were planes flying over
I don't remember really
Then the sailors with the pipes
Guns were fired
I think the national anthem was played
On top of the coffin there was a large wreath
Of white roses and small lilies from the Queen
And King George the VI's sword
Which he gave him when he married the Princess
And his admiral's hat
And they went into the Abbey, into the chapel
And placed the coffin on the purple catafalque I think they call it

He was buried in the vault with all the other people
You didn't see that
The service was written by the Duke
The hymns, the prayers, the psalms
The Deacon of Windsor carried out the service
And the Archbishop of Canterbury read the eulogy and gave a blessing
Music included
For those in peril on the sea
I vow to thee my country
The Queen sat alone on one side
On the other side Charles and Camilla
Then all the other Royals with no social distancing
A choir of three men and one soprano
They were social distanced
They were standing almost in the lobby of the chapel
At the end of the service the Scotsman with the bagpipes played a haunting tune
And there were four buglers
Played the last post
When they returned to the chapel
The coffin had disappeared and had been taken to the vaults
Mourners left the chapel
The Queen drove back to the castle in her car, in her limousine
Everyone else walked
Harry and William were walking either side of the Deacon and talking
They've got to make it up if possible haven't they

The tea
I imagined
Smoked salmon sandwiches
Egg and chives on home made bread
Home made on the premises
Cucumber
Miniature cakes
Cakes that you eat in two mouthfuls
I suppose covered with some kind of chocolate icing
Spongy things
Can you make a small mille-feuille?
Maybe a little palmier
Oh I expect Earl Grey or Darjeeling
The tea would come in a silver teapot
Nice china cups
If they were those shallow things they'd be hopeless
They don't even keep the tea hot
Anyway the Queen will be back to the State Opening of Parliament on Wednesday

She'll work her way though it
She'll keep busy
Go back to work
I don't think she'll ever live in Buckingham Palace again
A white elephant
Well they'll have banquets there won't they
Well when they have State dignitaries
Coming from abroad

Lunch Tea and Dinner

Hanna came for tea at 4 o'clock
And she left around quarter past 6
I don't know
After she left
I finished my lunch
Then I realised
It was ten to seven
Nearly time for dinner

What happened was
I made my lunch about half past two
Put it in the microwave
And left it on the table
With my lunchtime pills
Went to the bedroom
Felt tired
Lay down and fell asleep

The doorbell woke me up at 4 o'clock
So I thought
Well
By the time I got to the hall
There was a knock at the door
Somebody else had let her in
So I opened the door
My head was in a whirl
I said
Oh Hanna
I just woke up
She said
Shall I go home?
So I put her in the stairlift
Went back to put some shoes on
So I could accompany her
Down to the front door
But she couldn't have gone home
Because her carer had gone out with the keys
By that time I said
No you must come in
She was in the stairlift only about 5 mins
So she sat down and I made her a cup of tea
And some biscuits

And I took my lunch in
To eat in the sitting room

(I had the first half at half past 4
and the second half at half past 6)

So we were talking
And when she decided to go home
I walked down the stairs with her
She looked for her keys in her bag
And remembered that the carer had them
So she said
The people on the ground floor who have the keys are away
She wanted to go over the road to her door
I said you can't stand in the hall
So I tried to persuade her to sit in the stairlift in the hall
So then she phoned the carer
Who didn't answer
And I said
What a pity she hadn't looked in her bag for her keys
When she was in the sitting room
Then luckily there was a tap on the door and the carer was there
She'd been for a walk somewhere.
When she got home she phoned me
And said
I'm sitting here with a whiskey and a bag of crisps
And you know
While I was out the squirrel was in
He opened a packet of chocolate
And ate two whole pieces

Crab in the Hat

I left the surgery
And went to the fish shop
And bought some white crab meat
Came home
In the evening
I put a wrap in the microwave
Over a glass dish
Five minutes
It came out in the shape of a golden brown hat
Into which I put the crab meat
Chopped up lettuce
Tomato beetroot cucumber
Then I sat down and ate it
With a glass of white wine
It was delicious

Beach in the Bed

For the last couple of months
Every night when I go to bed
I lie with my head on the pillow
On my right side
And with my left hand
I smooth the sheet underneath
Which I call the beach
And tunnel my left hand under my pillow
To make a cave
Where I warm my hand
My palm and knuckle
Before settling down to sleep
Sometimes I move my hand
Further down the sand
And rest it there

Fairhazel Gardens

In 1970
When Genia was staying with us for Christmas
We all went to have tea with Eva Evagora
Suzy's friend from school
And her parents
At their flat in Fairhazel Gardens

Quite recently a nice young couple
John and Nadia
Carried my shopping home
From M&S
In West End Lane

They came up into the flat
And admired the plants
In the sittingroom window
And wrote down their mobile telephone number

Soon afterwards I realised
That I'd lost it and was very upset
They'd told me they lived on a corner
Somewhere in Fairhazel Gardens

So last Saturday
I took a cab down there
And put notes
Through several corner letterboxes

I was about to walk home
When I saw the house which Eva Evagora lived in
Now looking much smarter
With a white painted door
And white metal grilled windows

I walked up the path
To put a note through that door
And turned around to see them
Following me
We had a good laugh

They were as pleased to see me as I was them
They gave me their telephone number again

And said
Come for tea one day

New Paintings

I was going to do a picture of the ceiling
Of the rehab hospital
A dead butterfly and two dead flies
I will do it sometime
When I go into that room

I intend to paint the various objects on the divider
The pink vase from the hotel in Abano in Italy
From Murano
The hotel gave it to us when we checked out

I like the coffee pot
I'll never do it but
I like the cockerel down there
The coffee pot is from Gloucestershire
We rented a cottage
And went into an antique shop
About seven years ago

The pink cup
Suzy and Ricky bought from Poland
I'll be doing drawings and paintings
over the next few weeks

Shredded Wheat

During my telephone conversation
with Suzy this morning
I told her that I had eaten two shredded wheats
2 prunes and one apricot
(having asked my carer for 2 apricots and one prune)
and she said Richards' eyebrows were all over the place
I asked why
because he hadn't eaten shredded wheat since he was a child
I told Suzy to buy him a box
He can eat one dry and the other one pour hot milk over it
it makes a very good breakfast
You're not really cereal people are you
I told her
What is really?
I asked Suzy
I mean gramatically
It's not an adjective or a verb
I don't know said Suzy
It might be an adverb I said

The Hum

Sometimes when I have my head on the pillow
I hear a hum that goes hmmmm hmmmm hmmmm
I think it's somebody trying to speak to me
From outer space
I tried to reply
Who is it?
What do you want to say to me?
And I imagine that they go
hmmuhhhummmuhmm hmmuhhhummmuhmm
humming up and down

You can't hear the up and down when you write it

My Diligence Mark

I was coming to school in the morning
and I saw mushrooms
growing in the playing field
so I picked them and went to the cloakroom
and was putting them in my pocket
they thought we didn't know the difference
between mushrooms and puffballs
or anything poisonous
when the biology teacher
(who was a lesbian
and a lot of the girls including me had a crush on her
she had short boyish hair
a pink leather jacket
a brown tartan skirt
and rather frumpy brown stockings and shoes)
had obviously followed me after seeing what I had done
saw me putting them in my pocket
She said, "What are you doing June?
You know you have to take them to Miss Davies the cookery teacher."
She walked away and left me
and I only took half of them to Miss Davies
I went to the classroom
The biology teacher Miss Short
She came in
and told me to go to the headmistress
Miss Appleton
who gave me a diligence mark
(three diligence marks in one term and girls could be expelled)
So she reprimanded me and gave me an essay to write
in detention time after school hours entitled
The importance of obedience to authority in a democracy

I went home and discussed it with my mother
And we sat down and decided what to say
She probably wrote the essay
And I put it in my own words
Later the headmistress called me to her office
And congratulated me
Said it was very good
I have told this story many times
And often wished when telling this story
That I had brought it home

But wouldn't you think
that very shortly afterwards
it would have been torn up and thrown away?

My Other Detention

I had another detention
Chemistry
In each lesson we carried out experiments
Preparation
then
Result
Books were handed in every week and I had spelt preparation
PREPERATION
The chemistry teacher had put a red line through the E
But she hadn't said what it should be
The following week I did it again
Consequently I received a detention

The Ostrich

You and I collected an ostrich
From a zoo in Victoria Street
And went into Victoria Station
And took a train to Petts Wood

Karen and Jo were there
We stayed the night
And I don't remember what we ate
Or feeding the ostrich

We all caught the train
Back to Victoria Station
With the ostrich on a lead
The ostrich was always in the guards van

You left
And I went into a smart restaurant
Which was empty
Except for a man and his wife
The man was served a steak
In a creamy bubbling sauce
With nothing else
And his wife had three light boiled eggs
Also in a creamy sauce
I ordered the same thing
The eggs
But never got to eat them
Because I woke up

In the restaurant
The ostrich was under the table
With his head on my lap
I took the ostrich back to the zoo
He was still there
I walked him back
I never saw the door of the zoo
Or the other animals
I must have handed him over to a keeper

I've kept this in my head for two days
Repeating it to myself
In case I forget it

Car Number Plates

Suzy has asked me to paint a picture
Of the cars
With the colour
Of the back of the boot
Green Austin – KUU 96Z/2
(new car overtook the KUU)
Blue Honda – SYL 532
Toyota Estate (brown) – RYK 599R
Once stolen with only a box of mineral water in it
The wine had already been taken upstairs
To the flat
The Police couldn't find it
Even though it had been parked
Around the corner from the police station
Our garage repair man found it
Because he was familiar with it

Hanukkah Tea Party

Helen came with me instead of Zissi
Because she had never been to a party like that before
The first thing I noticed was the dark haired lady
With slight dementia
Accompanied by a carer and friend
Both looking very concerned about her welfare
She had obviously made a great effort
To come there today
And left without eating or drinking anything
I felt she would soon leave this world
How sad
She was no more than 80 years old

The usual sandwiches were on the plates
Smoked salmon, egg and onion
And tea of course
The magnolia tree in the garden
Is a sight to behold

One of the doormen had hailed us a black cab
To take us home for supper at Compayne

Memories of 23 Bracknell Gardens NW3
Twice someone came into the flat at night
Once I woke up to see a man
Poking his head round the door
Probably thinking it was a house
And that he was in a living room
When I got up in the morning
I found ten shillings had been taken out of my purse
On the hall table

The next time someone had climbed
Through the side window and also taken
Ten shillings from my purse
Next time a very small person crawled through
The small window in the pantry
And taken my handbag from the armchair
Beside the fireplace
The French au pair rushed to see
If her passport was still there
It was Nadia

Who went home to France
Because her father was unwell

The garden was delightful
And there was a pile of sand for Suzy to play with
The Italian gardener was there bringing plants in May
To put in the tubs and side flower beds
Suzy's painting of her father with a profile of her child's face
Is a painting of the garden too

The garden at No. 8 was not a patch on No. 23
We had a white rabbit in a hutch
The greengrocer at the top of West End Lane
kept us supplied with green lettuce etc.

An Apparition

I woke up one night
Saw a small old woman
With a wrinkled face and dress
Standing by the bed
And looking down at me

She must be another
Ghost of 63a Compayne Gardens
She did not go away
Like the previous lady
I screamed very loudly
I rang
Yes I remember well
I rang 6 times
But my carer
I don't remember
Which one it was
Failed to come
And see what the noise
Was about
I went to sleep
At 7am she had dropped
Into 'thin air'

Singing Talent

I was invited to sing
at "London Got Talent"
You know I can't sing
a note don't you
Far cry from Susan
Brown who won the
Contest one year and
Became a millionairess
But still lives in her council
House with same lifestyle

My mother was a soprano
And used to sing the
Floral Dance at the
Family Christmas party
My sister was a contralto
And Mum used to say I
Sang like Alice Faye an
Actress and singer in the
1940s

My Father's Shed

Playhouse
96 Rushmere Road 1935 - 1960

The shed was wood
It had a concrete step
Lino floor with a mat
A bench to sit on under the window
With a long cushion nailed on
A table with a tablecloth
And a small glass vase with flowers
There was a window with curtains, cotton
Outside on the grass was a hammock
And an apple tree
The apples were pink and yellow
(I never tasted anything like it)
And on the wooden fence at the end of the garden
Pink and white tea roses
Further along to the right
Lilies of the valley
A lovely perfume
Father used to send me some
In a box
First to the Seymour Street flat
And then to Bracknell Gardens

Rushmere, the bungalow 1960

When my parents moved to the bungalow
In Rushmere
Harry Weavers dismantled the shed
And moved it on a lorry to the garden
Of the bungalow and
Erected it for Dad
He used to do a lot of woodwork
And he had all these OXO tins
Nailed to the wall under the window
Where he kept nails and screws
He made a crib board
A bookshelf for Suzy

When we were living at the shop

People living at a house opposite
Said “Come quickly
Father is going to hang himself”
When he got there the man had
Already done it
Father had to cut him down
And call the Police I expect

The other side
Number 98
“Mr Scott come quickly
Father's locked himself in the bedroom
And he won't come out”
So father climbed up to the window
On a ladder
Climbed in and opened the door
Now opposite, also
Was a man called Reggie Grainger
About 28 years old
With smoothed down ginger hair
And glasses
He had a fiancé but on Saturday afternoons
He used to come over
To the shop and ask my mother and father
If he could take me to the cinema
We always went to the Ritz
In the Buttermarket
Where there was also the Ancient House
Where there was a secret panel
In the wood wall
Where Charles II hid during the War of the Roses

Further along the road was
Miller and Steels where my father worked
And learnt how to roast coffee
He used to tell us about Edward VII or VIII?
Who abdicated
He used to be escorted by police motorcycles
To Felixstowe to visit Mrs Simpson
In a rented house up on the cliffs there
I didn't know what happened to
Mrs Simpson in America

Changes

From Shag Pile
To Wood Floors
From Avocado Basins and Baths
To Walk In Showers

Ladybird Books and Pinking Shears

Do you remember Ladybird books
And pinking shears

They were used for cutting up material for
The rag books

Which Ladybird books can you remember?

I'd like to know what titles they did

Mothers used to read them to children
Peter Rabbit eating the lettuces

Run rabbit run rabbit run run run run
Don't give the farmer his fun fun fun
He'll get by
Without his rabbit pie
So run rabbit run rabbit run run run

The Messerschmitts over Ipswich used to go
errrhhhhh errrhhhhh errrhhhhh
and the English Lancaster bombers went
mmmmmm mmmmmmm mmmmmmm
We had the fighters
The ones that used to try and fire bomb the bombers
But it was ok
We had a Morrison metal table
Underneath there was a cage
Where you could put a mattress

If the house came down
The bricks wouldn't come in on you
But they hardly bombed Ipswich

Jack in the beanstalk
What was that about?
There were giants somewhere
Weren't there

And there's
Ladybird ladybird fly away home
Your house is on fire and your children are dead

Do you remember the May bugs?

In May they go zoom zoom

They'll go into your hair
My mother and Jackie couldn't bear them

We used to have marzipan ones
With paper feet

ARTWORKS

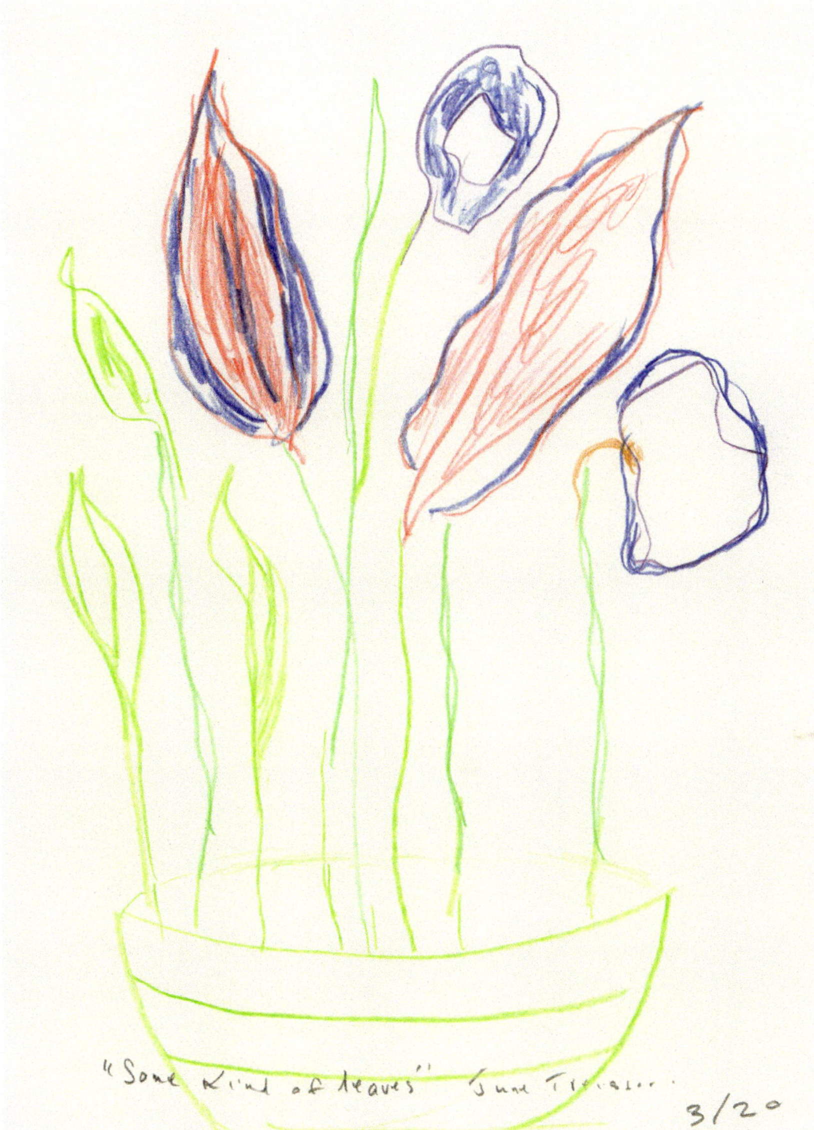

Some Kind of Leaves Coloured pencils on paper 29.7 x 21cm March 2020

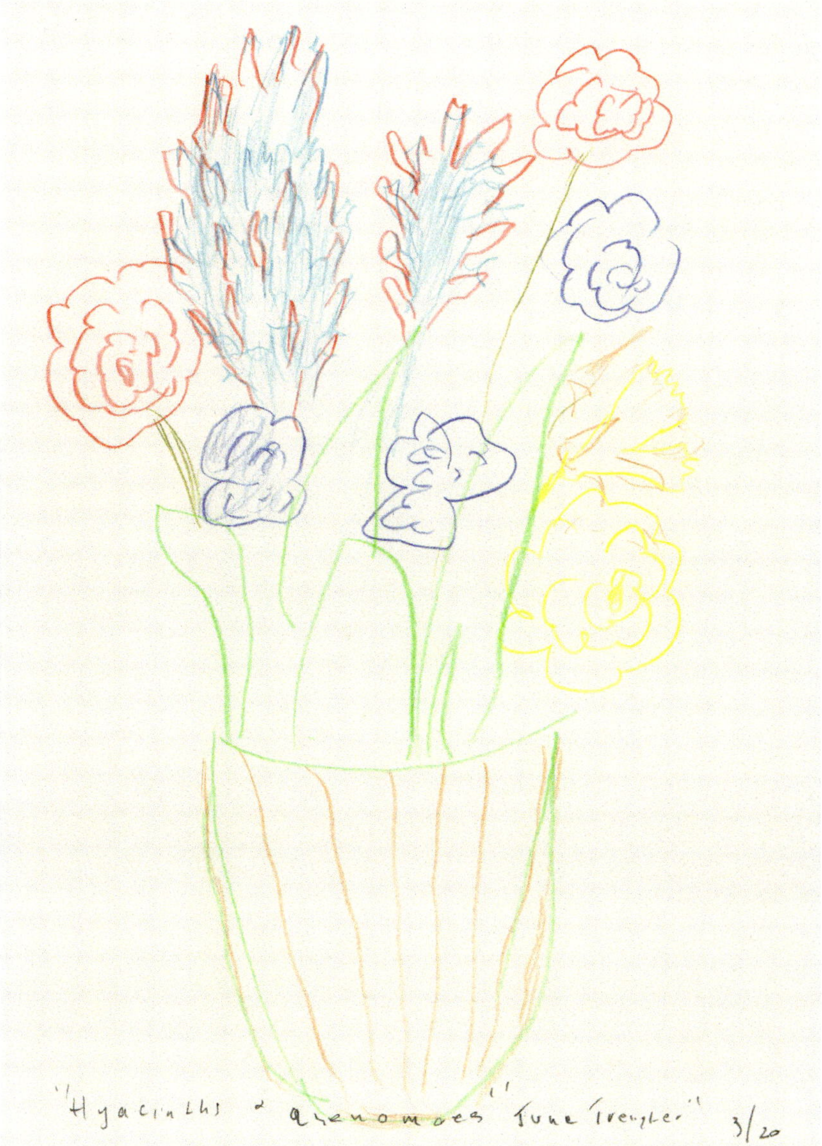

Hyacinths and Anemones Coloured pencils on paper 29.7 x 21cm March 2020

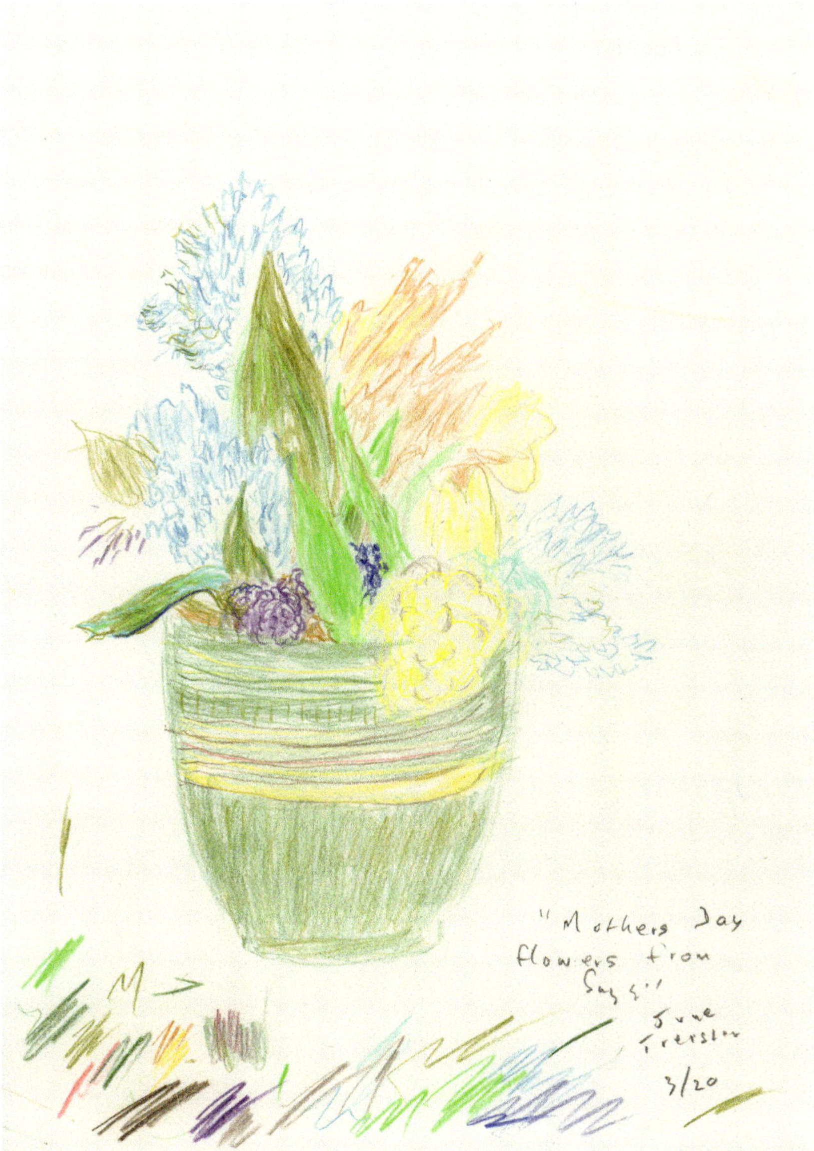

Mother's Day Flowers Coloured pencils on paper 29.7 x 21cm March 2020

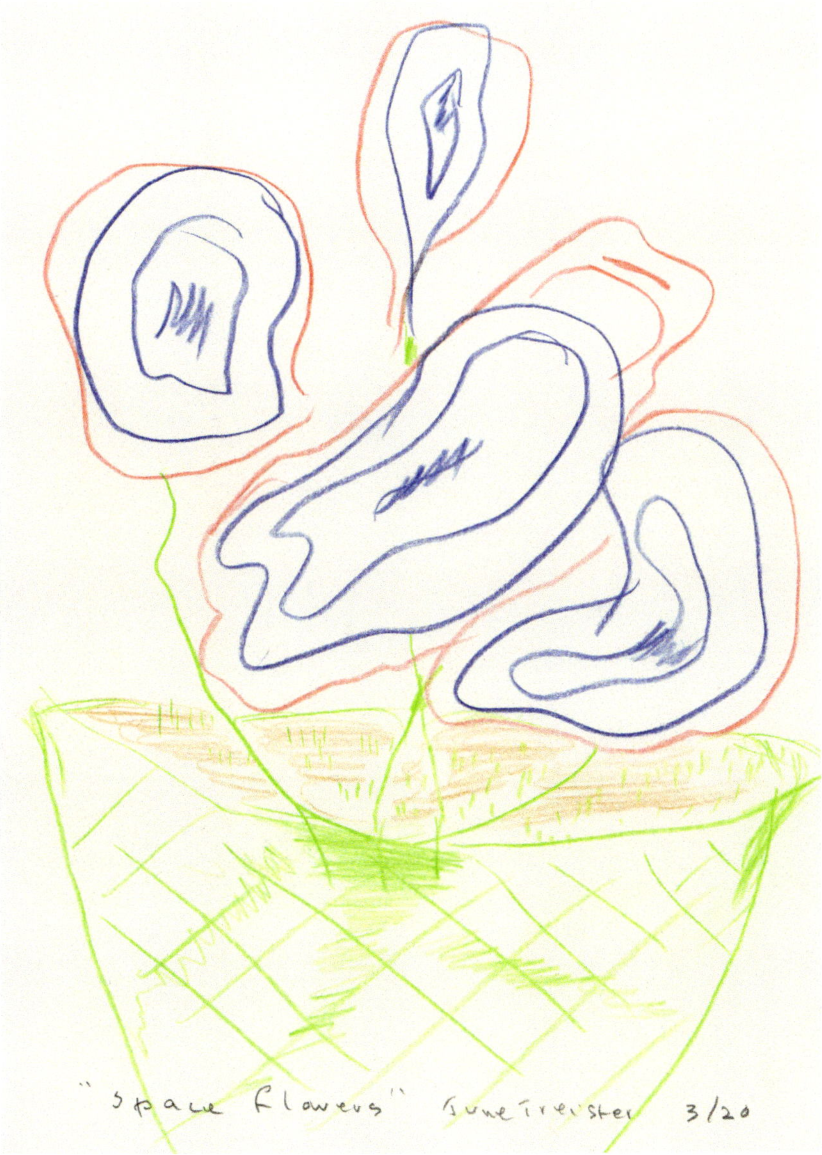

Space Flowers Coloured pencils on paper 29.7 x 21cm March 2020

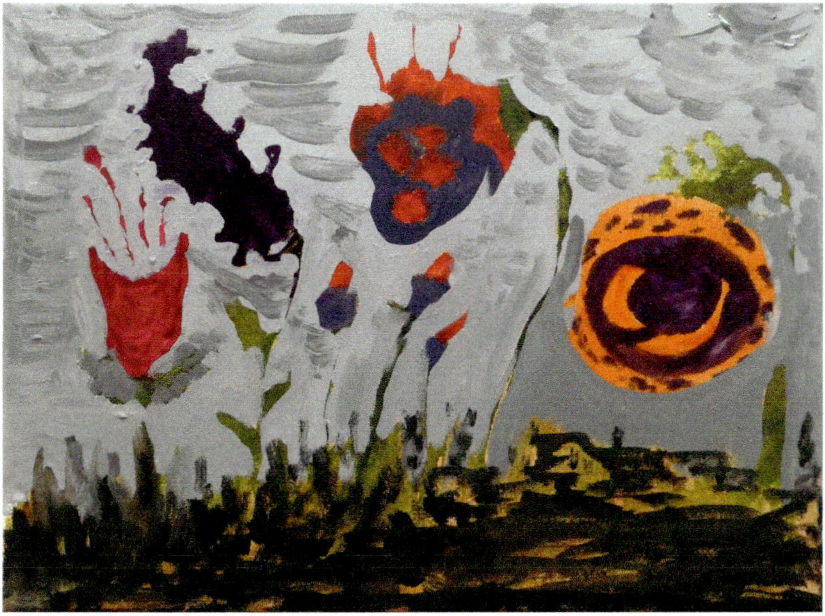

Space Flowers 1 Oil on canvas 30 x 40 cm April 2020

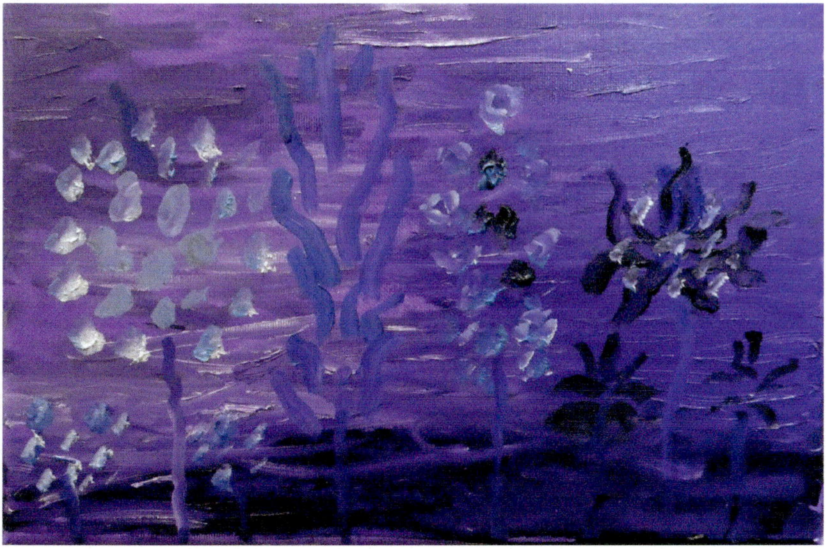

Blue Space Flowers Oil on canvas 20 x 30 cm April 2020

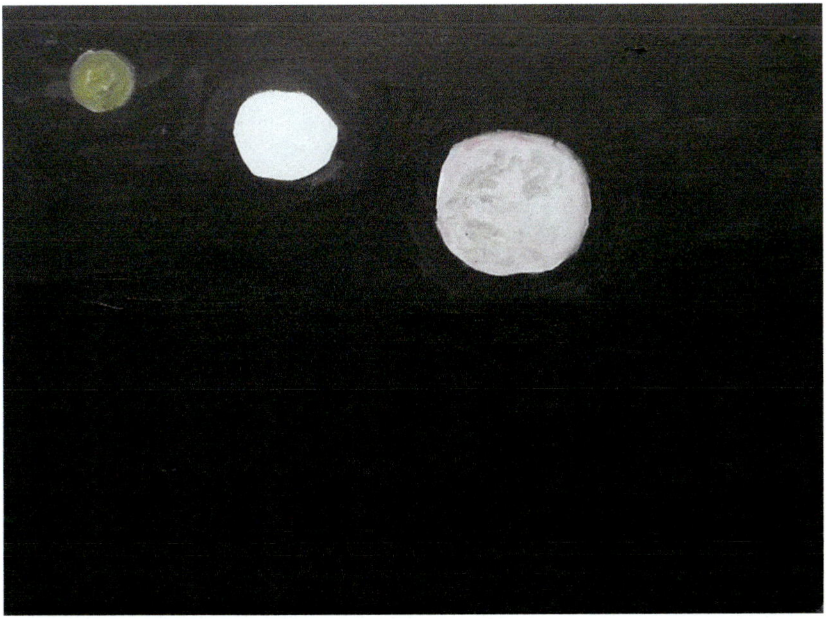

Three Moons Oil on canvas 30 x 40 cm April 2020

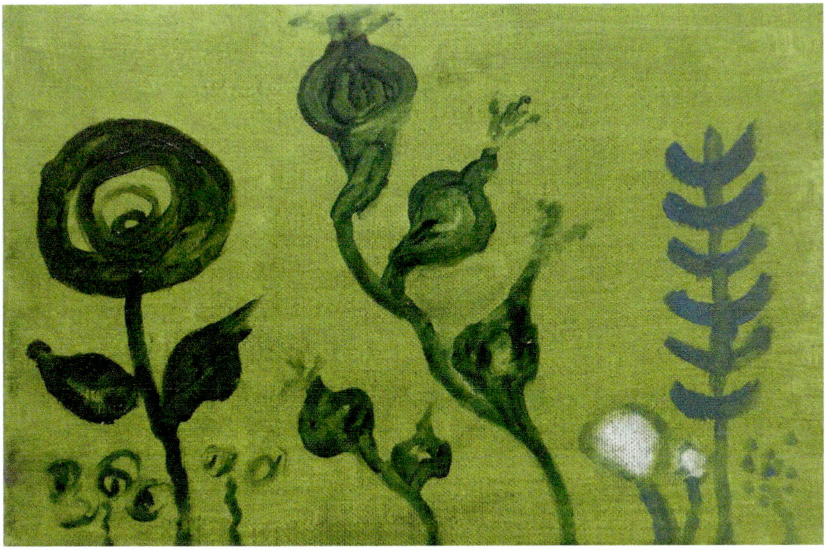

Green Space Flowers Oil on canvas 20 x 30 cm April 2020

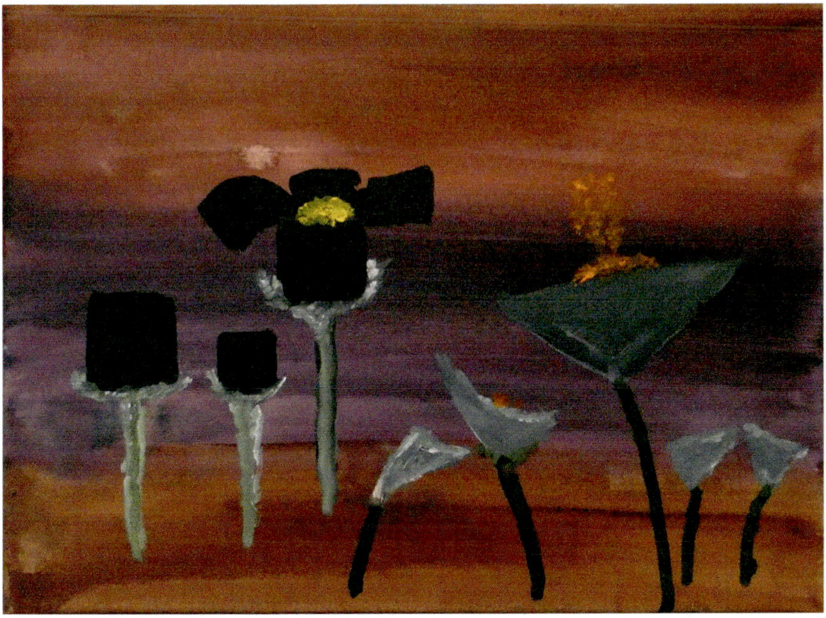

Square and Triangular Space Flowers Oil on canvas 30 x 40 cm April 2020

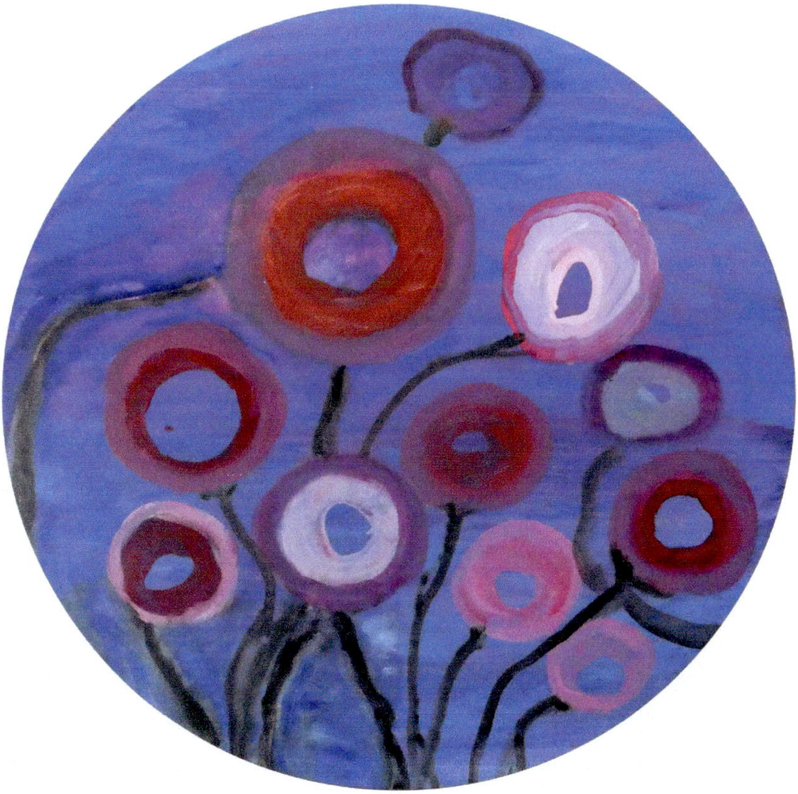

Circular Space Flowers Oil on canvas 30 cm diameter May 2020

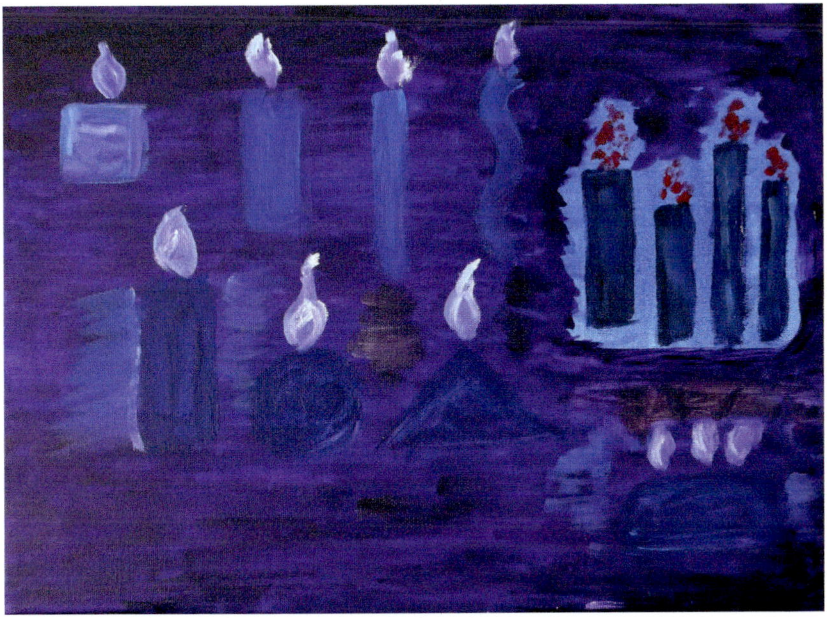

Space Candles Oil on canvas 30 x 40 cm June 2020

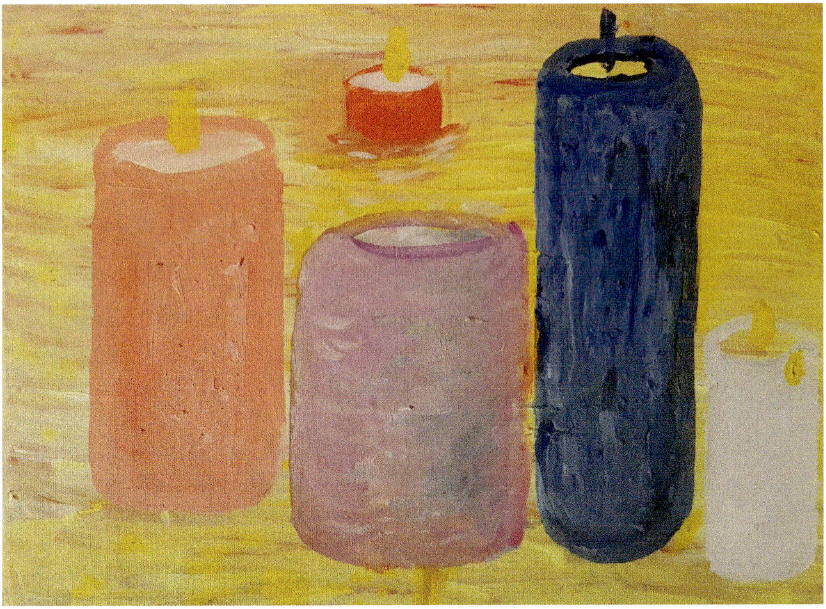

Space Candles 2 Oil on canvas 30 x 40 cm July-August 2020

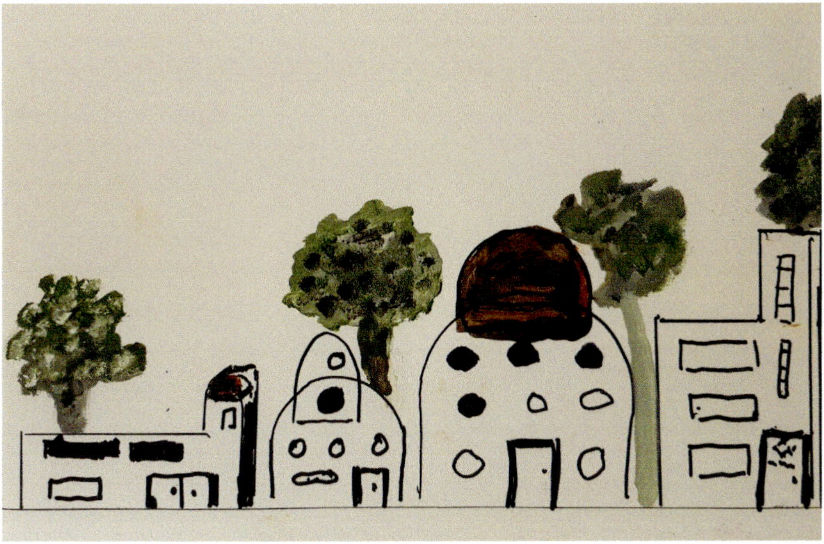

Space Village Oil on board 20 x 30 cm August 2020

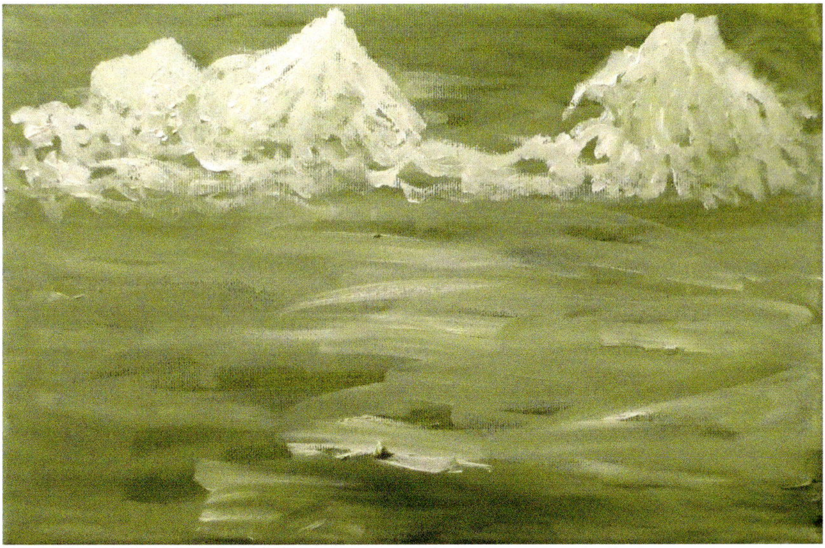

Mountains Oil on canvas 20 x 30 cm August 2020

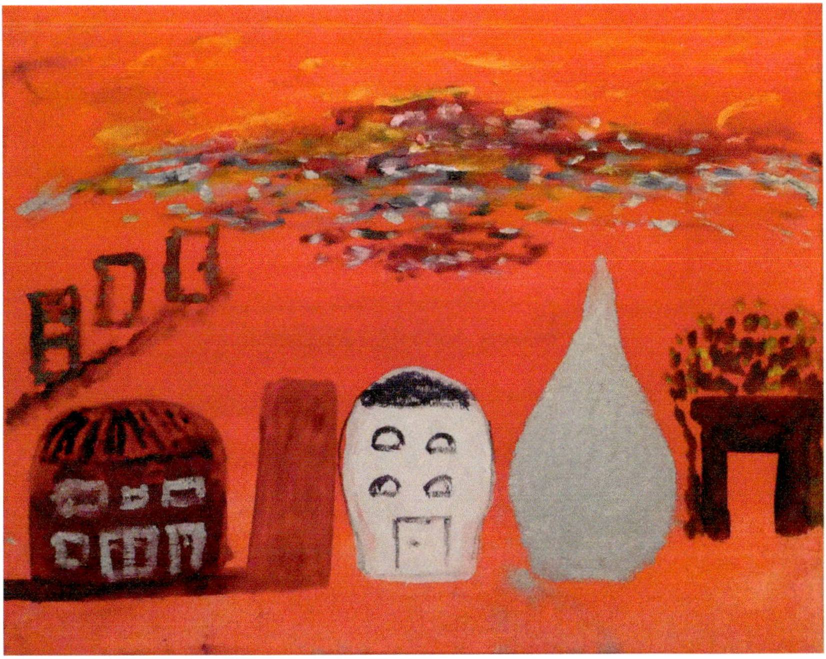

Space City Oil on canvas 40 x 50 cm September 2020

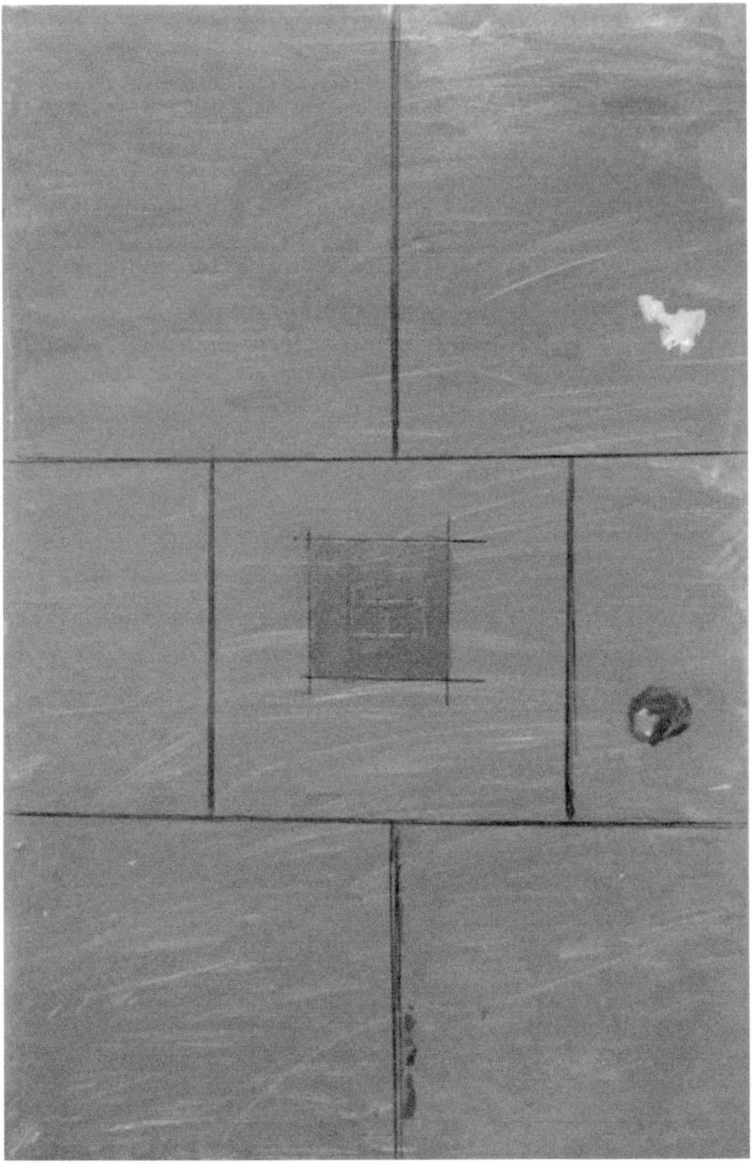

London Pavement with Tissue, Coffee Cup and Utility Hole Cover
Oil on board 30.5 x 19.5 cm January 2021

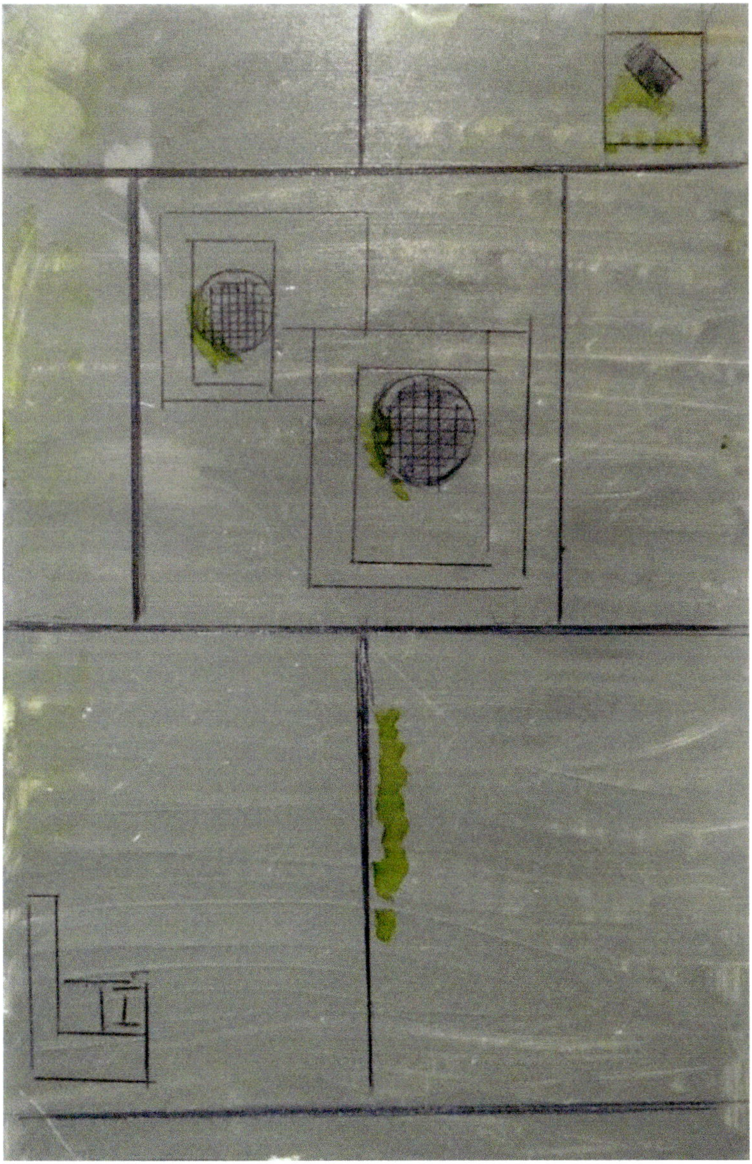

London Pavement with Utility Hole Covers Oil on board 30.5 x 19.5 cm January 2021

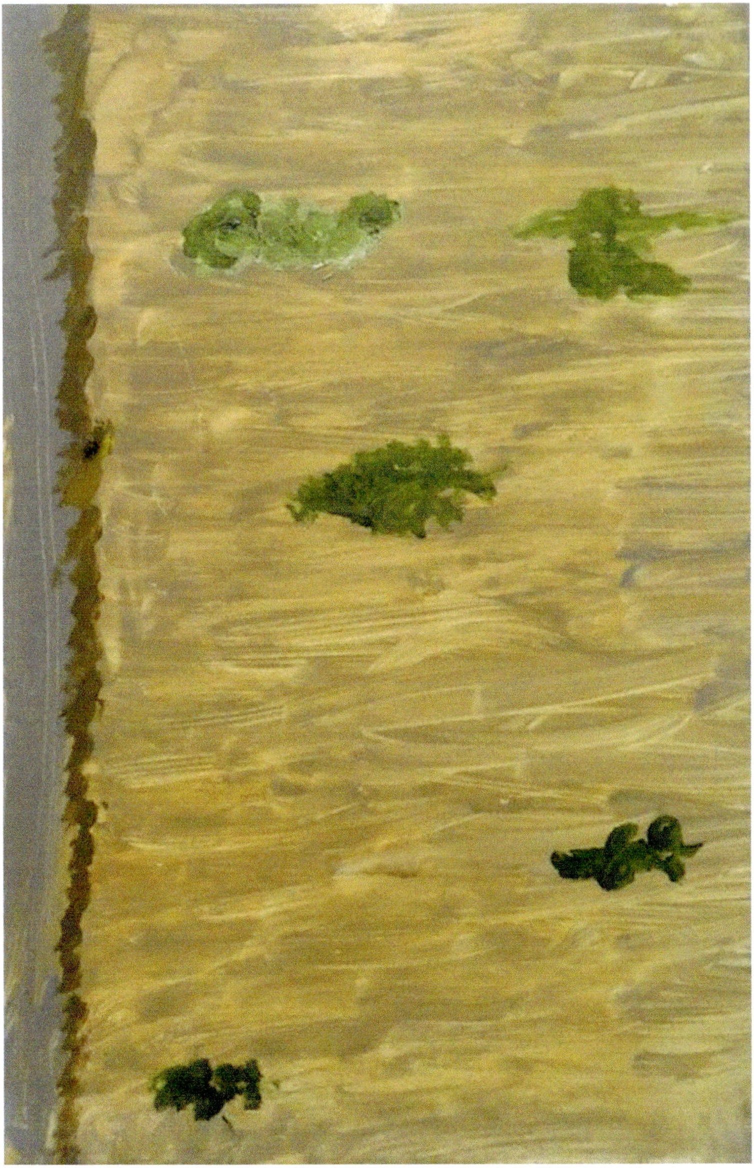

Country Lane with Moss Oil on board 30.5 x 19.5 cm January 2021

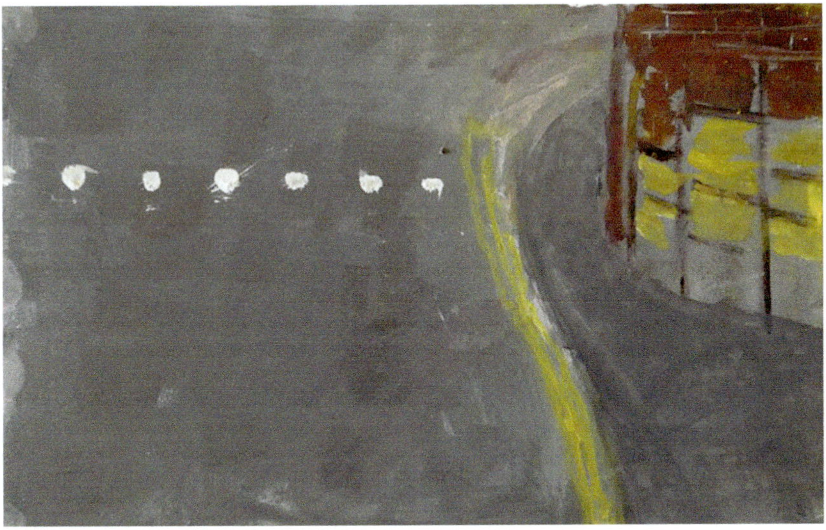

London Pavement - Corner of Broadhurst Gardens Oil on board 30.5 x 19.5 cm January 2021

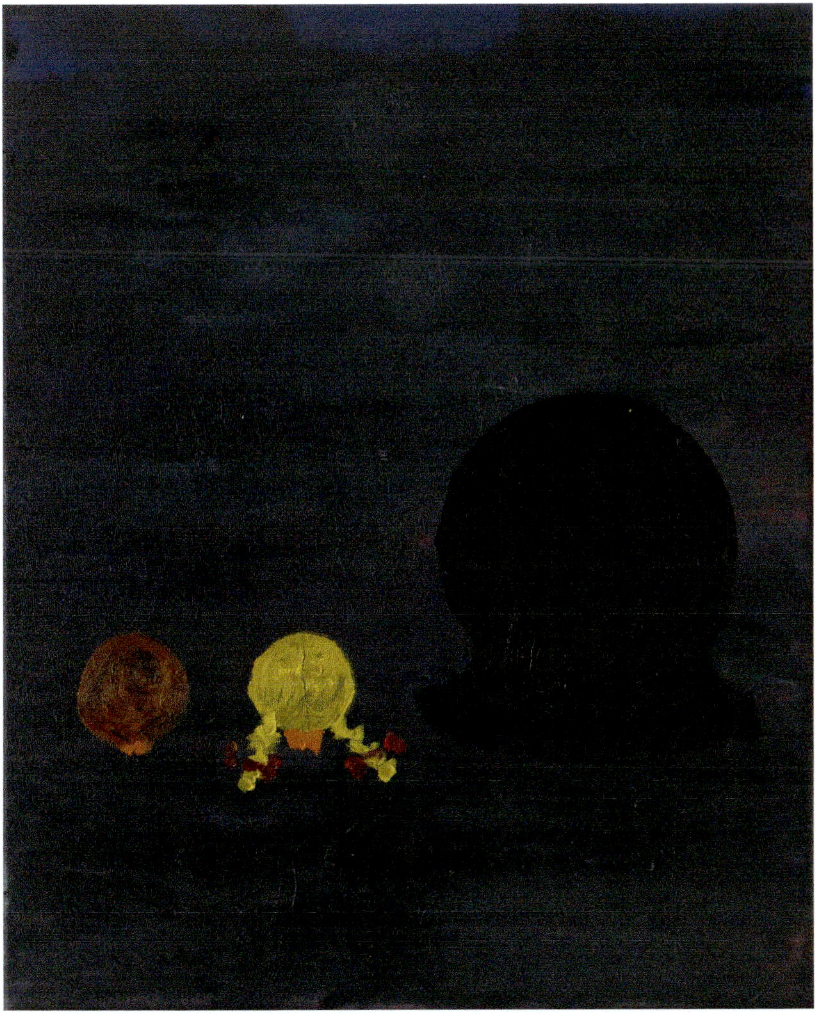

Pandemic Oil on canvas 40 x 50 cm February 2021

Palette Trouser Monoprints
A series of 12 works
March 2021

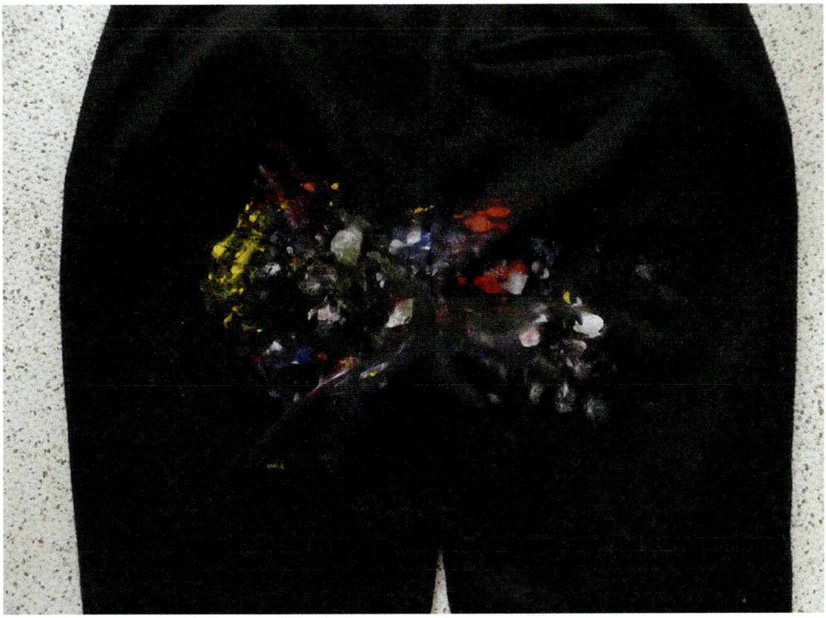

Not long ago my palette was on the chair and by mistake I sat in it.
I took some photographs of my trousers before I washed them.

Later it seemed a good idea to do this again and make some prints on paper.

For some of them I wiggled around and for others I slid down the paper which gave a completely different picture.

It was fun doing it and I was surprised and pleased with the results.

Palette Trouser Monoprint 1 Oil on paper 29.7 x 42 cm March 2021

Palette Trouser Monoprint 2 Oil on paper 29.7 x 42 cm March 2021

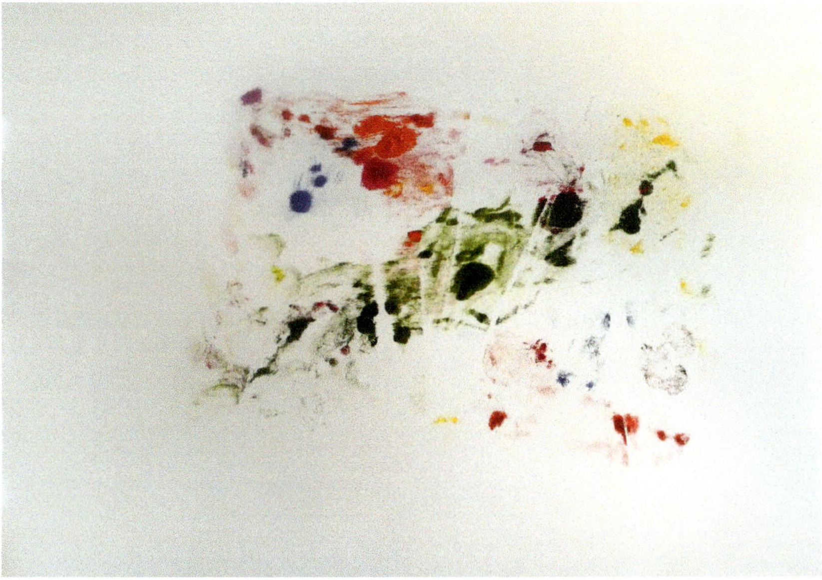

Palette Trouser Monoprint 3 Oil on paper 29.7 x 42 cm March 2021

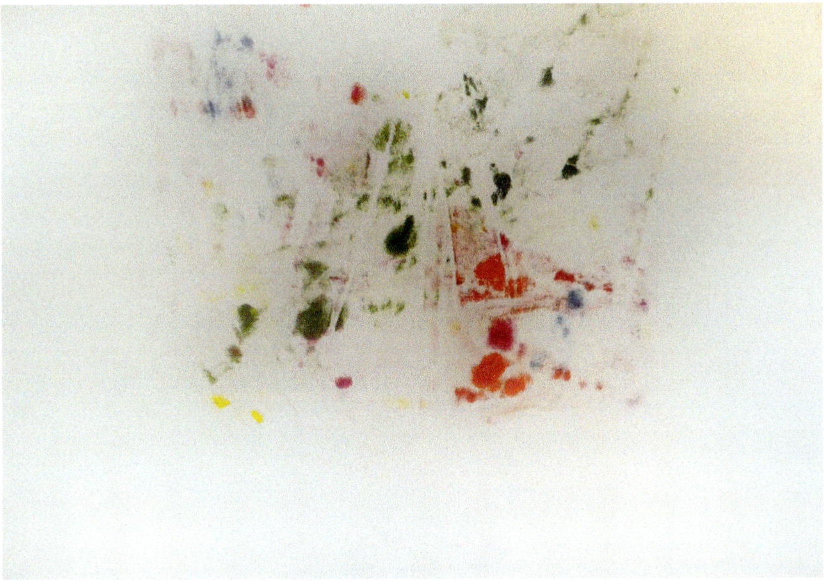

Palette Trouser Monoprint 4 Oil on paper 29.7 x 42 cm March 2021

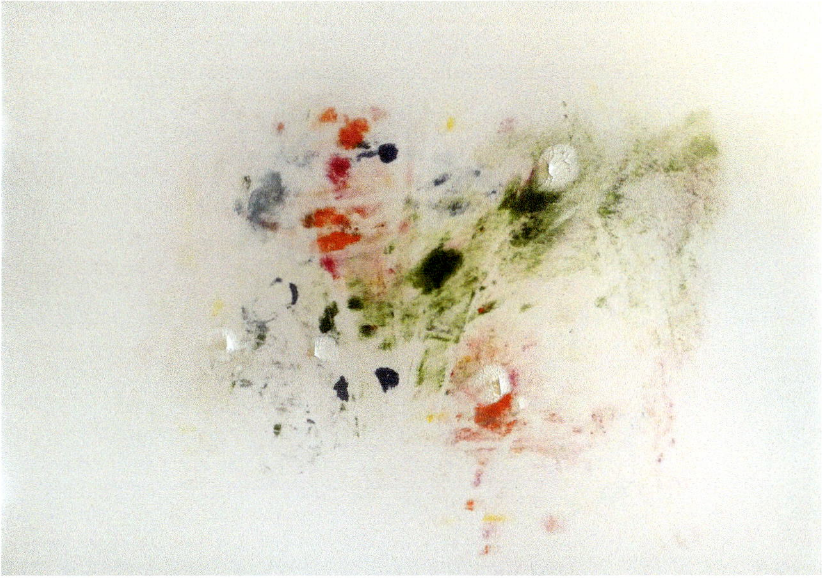

Palette Trouser Monoprint 5 Oil on paper 29.7 x 42 cm March 2021

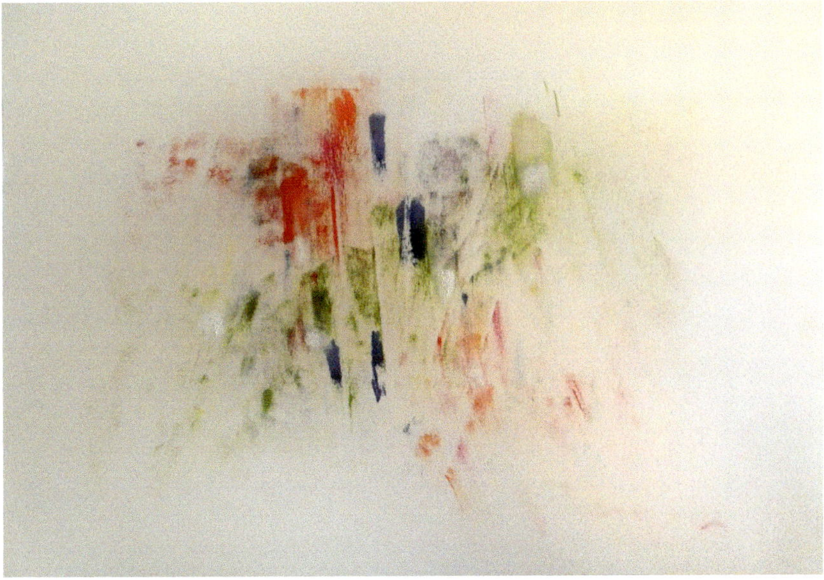

Palette Trouser Monoprint 6 Oil on paper 29.7 x 42 cm March 2021

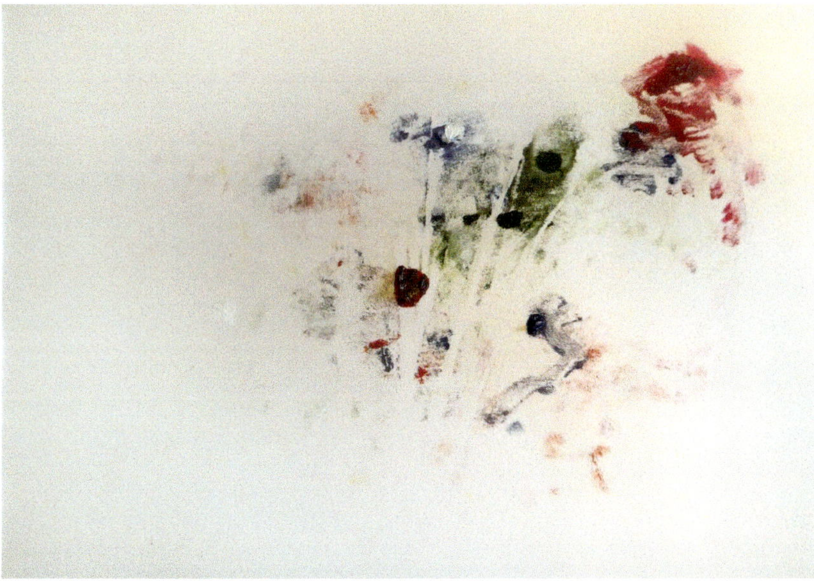

Palette Trouser Monoprint 7 Oil on paper 29.7 x 42 cm March 2021

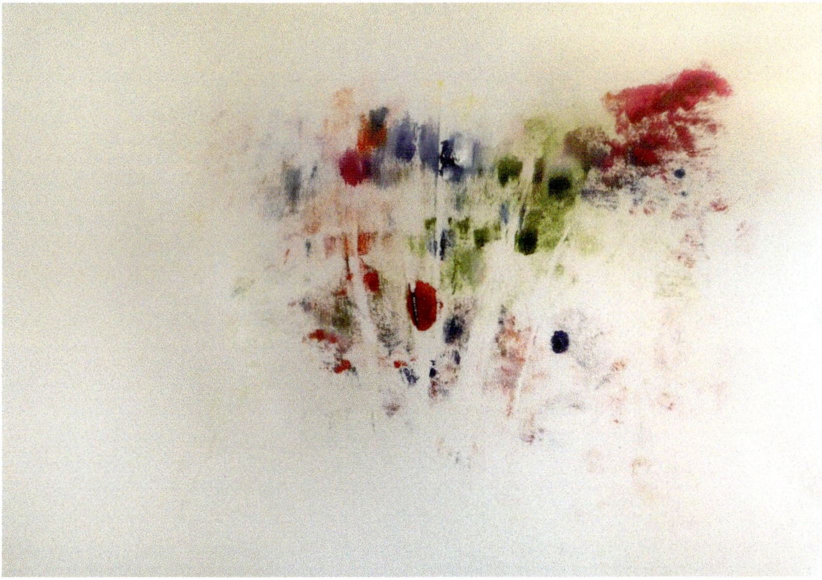

Palette Trouser Monoprint 8 Oil on paper 29.7 x 42 cm March 2021

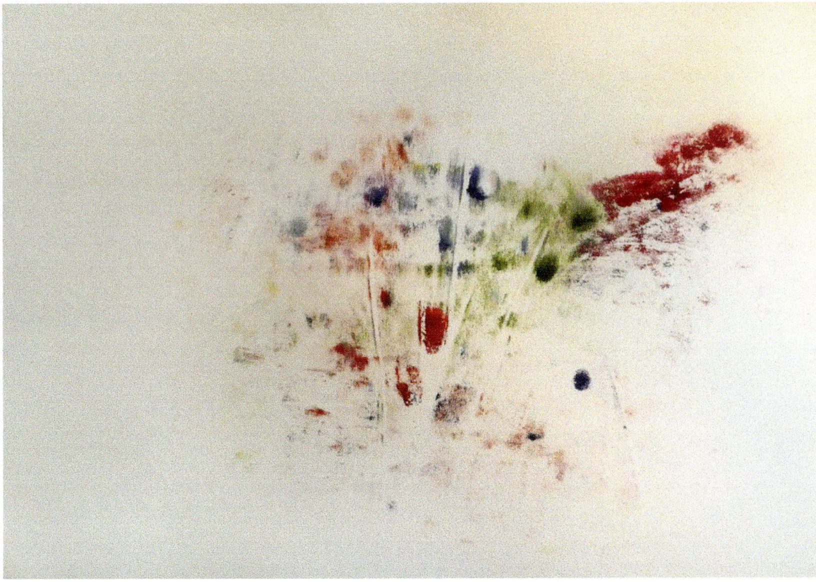

Palette Trouser Monoprint 9 Oil on paper 29.7 x 42 cm March 2021

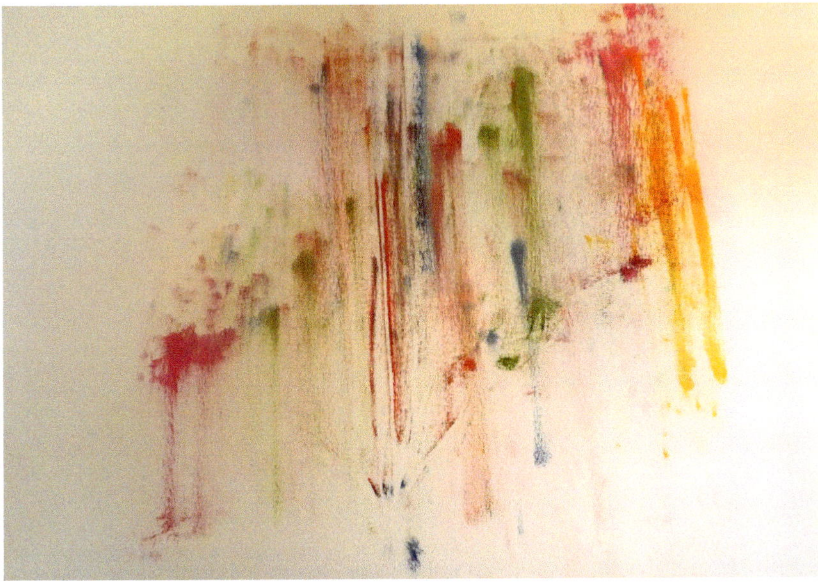

Palette Trouser Monoprint 10 Oil on paper 29.7 x 42 cm March 2021

Palette Trouser Monoprint 11 Oil on paper 29.7 x 42 cm March 2021

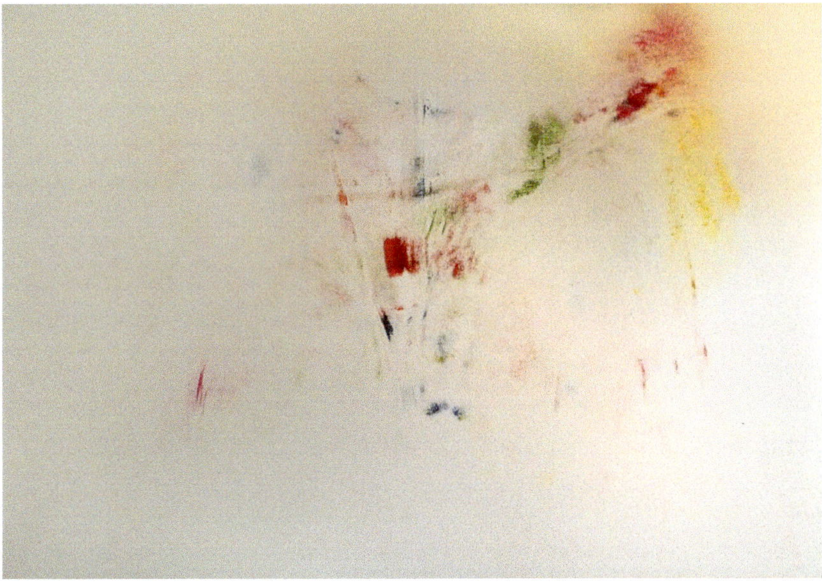

Palette Trouser Monoprint 12 Oil on paper 29.7 x 42 cm March 2021

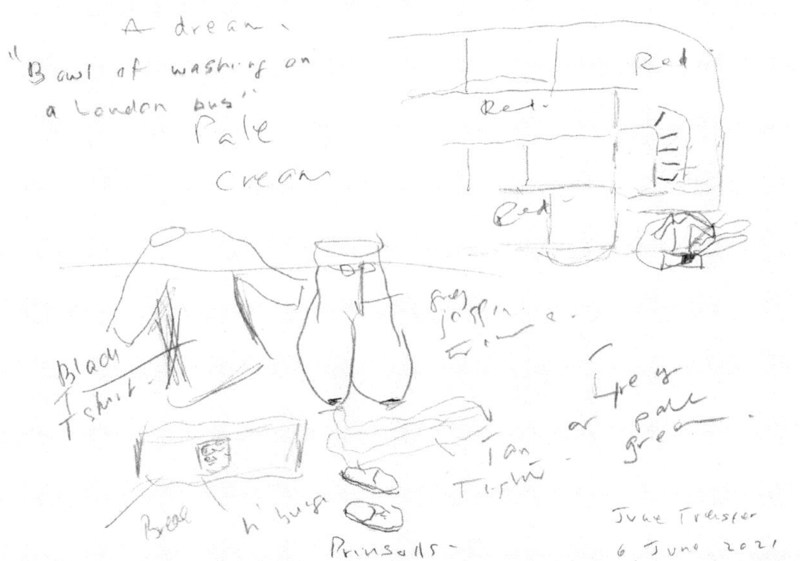

Dream Drawing: Bowl of Washing on a London Bus Pencil on paper 21 x 29.7 cm June 2021

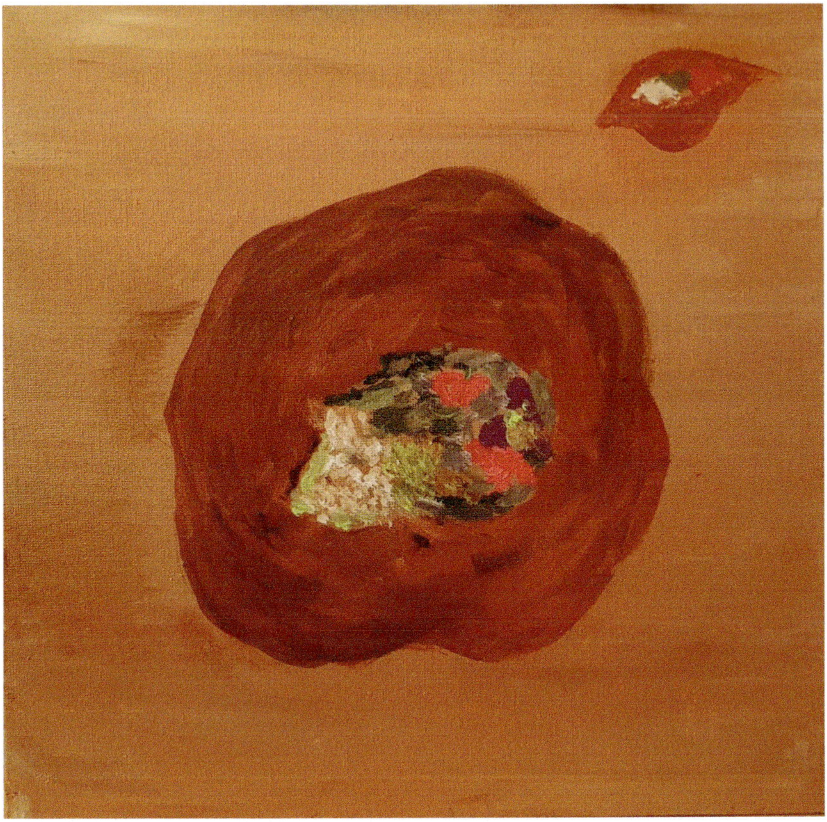

Crab in the Hat Oil on canvas board 30 x 30 cm August 2021

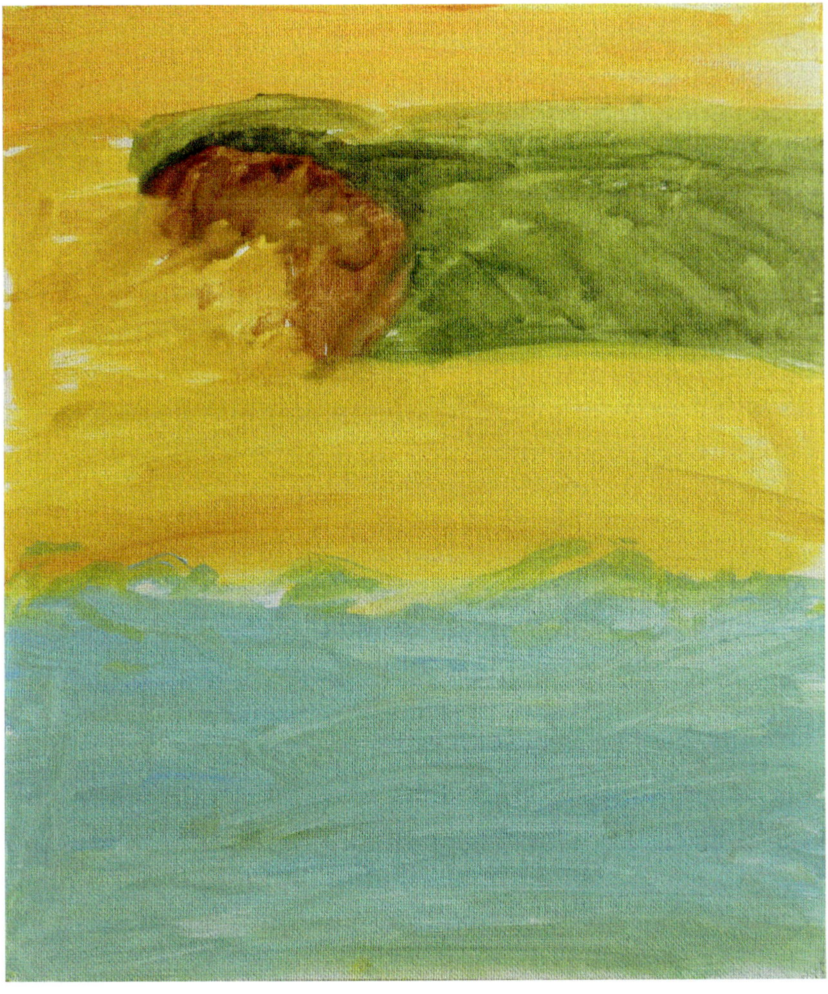

Beach in the Bed Oil on canvas board 12" x 10" October 2021

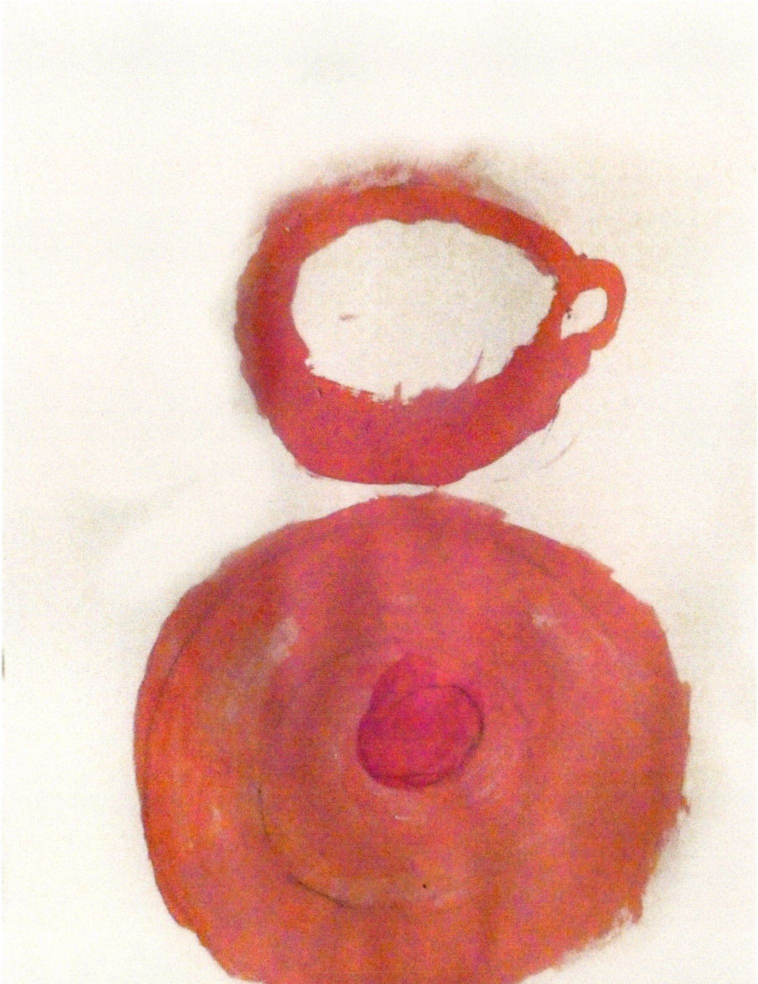

Pink Polish Cup Acrylic on paper 30.5 x 19.5 cm April 2022

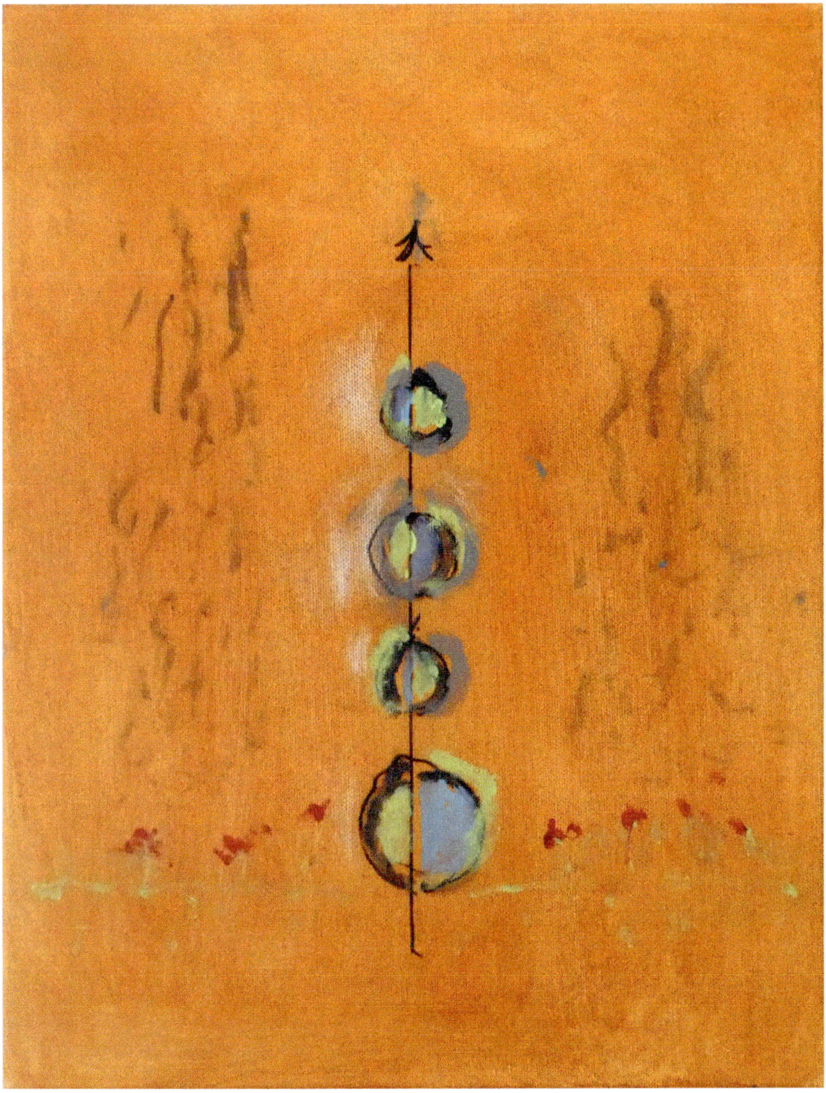

June's Painting of Suzy's Tree of Life Acrylic on canvas 40 x 30 cm May 2022

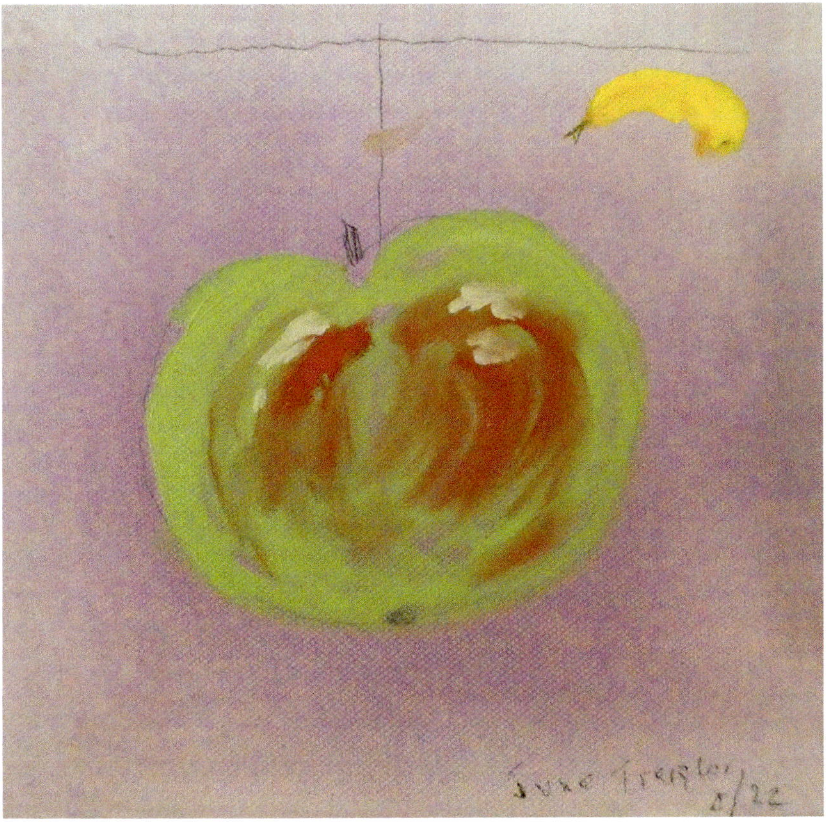

Hanging Apple and Banana Oil on canvas 20 x 20 cm August 2022

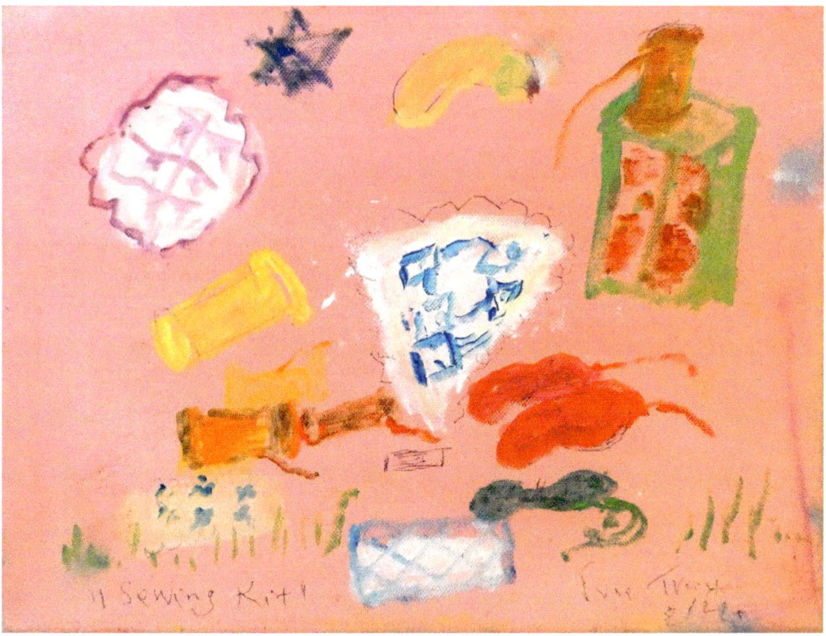

Sewing Kit Oil on canvas 35 x 27 cm August 2022

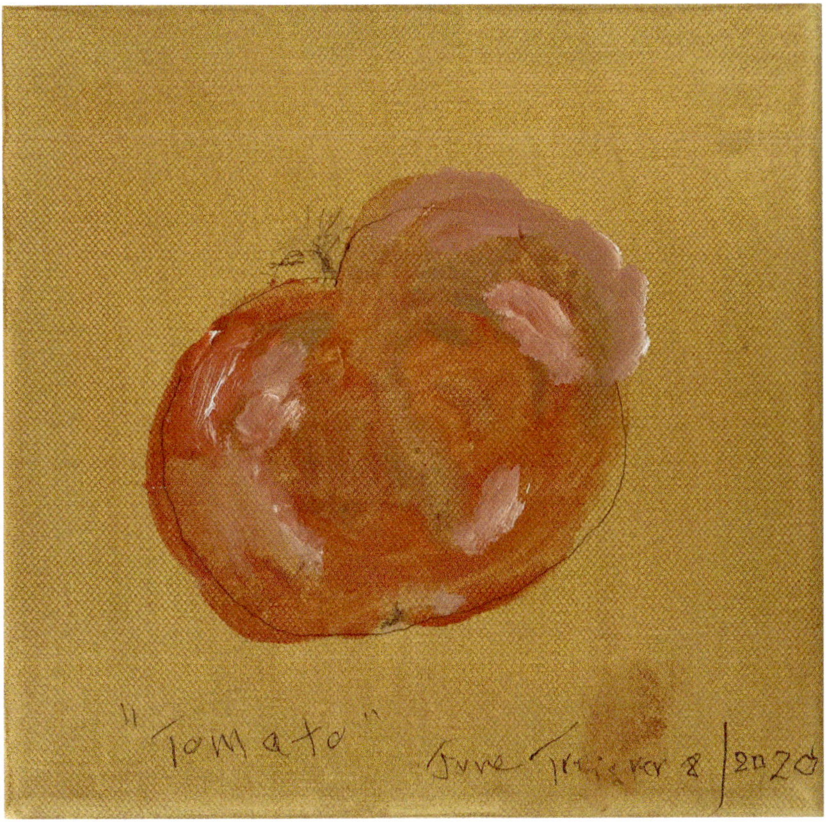

Tomato Oil on canvas 20 x 20 cm August 2022

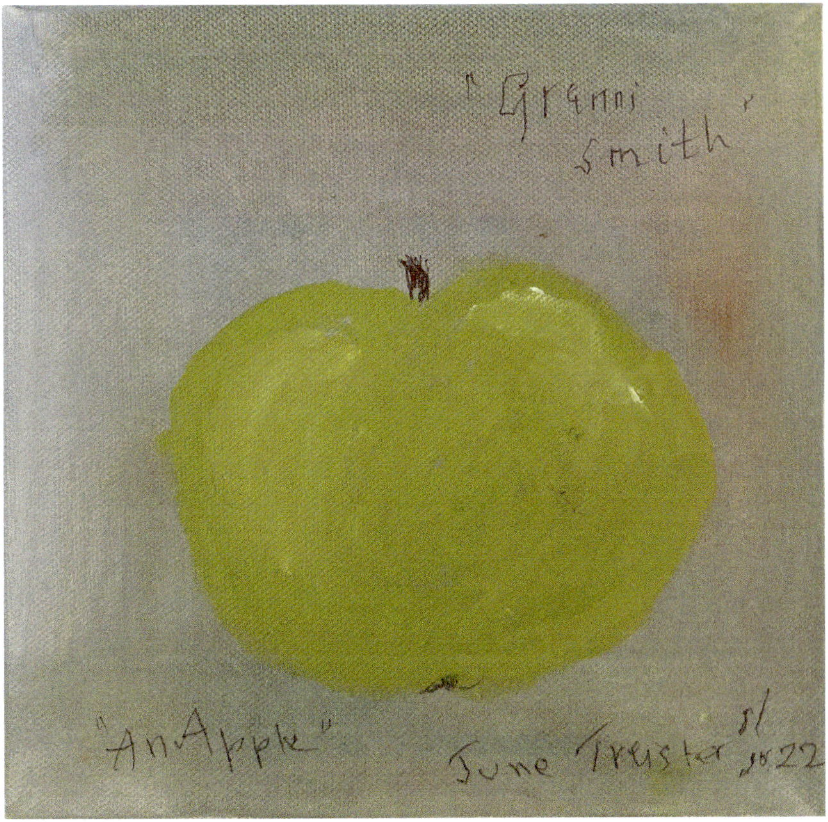

Granny Smith - An Apple Oil on canvas 20 x 20 cm August 2022

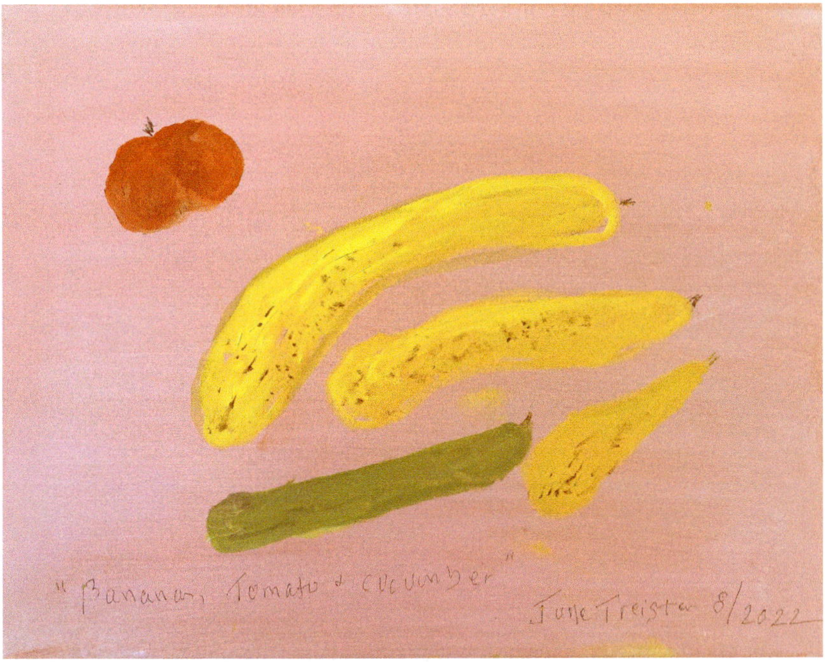

Bananas, Tomato and Cucumber Oil on canvas 33 x 41 cm August 2022
Collection Daniel Muzyczuk and Agnieszka Pindera

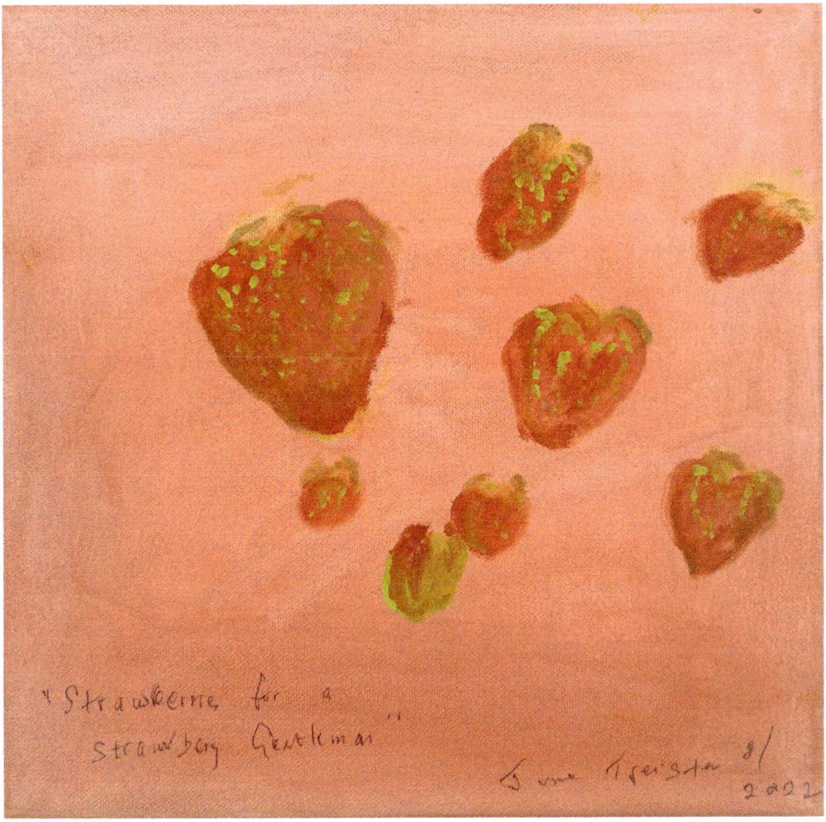

Strawberries for a Strawberry Gentleman Oil on canvas 30 x 30 cm August 2022
Collection Michael Boe

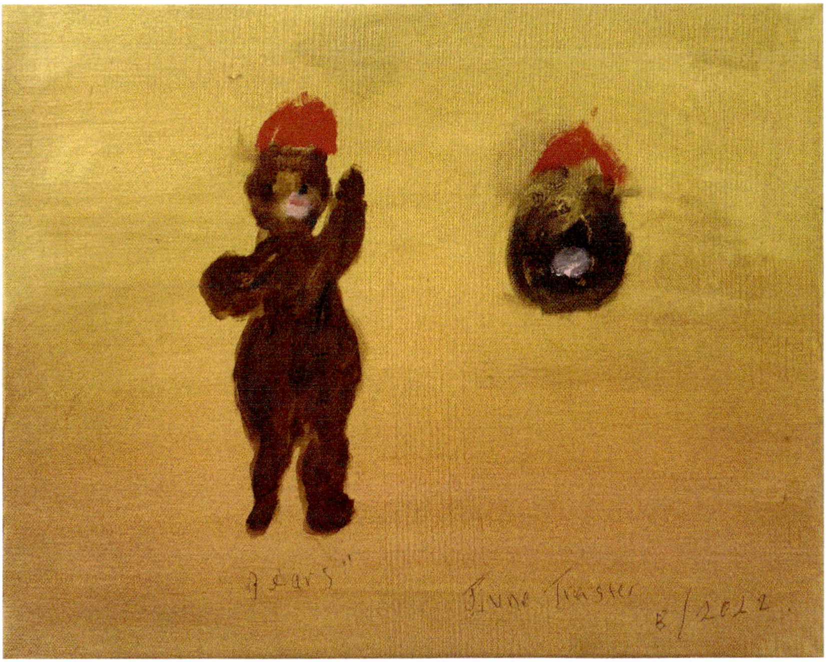

Bears 1 Oil on canvas 33 x 41 cm August 2022

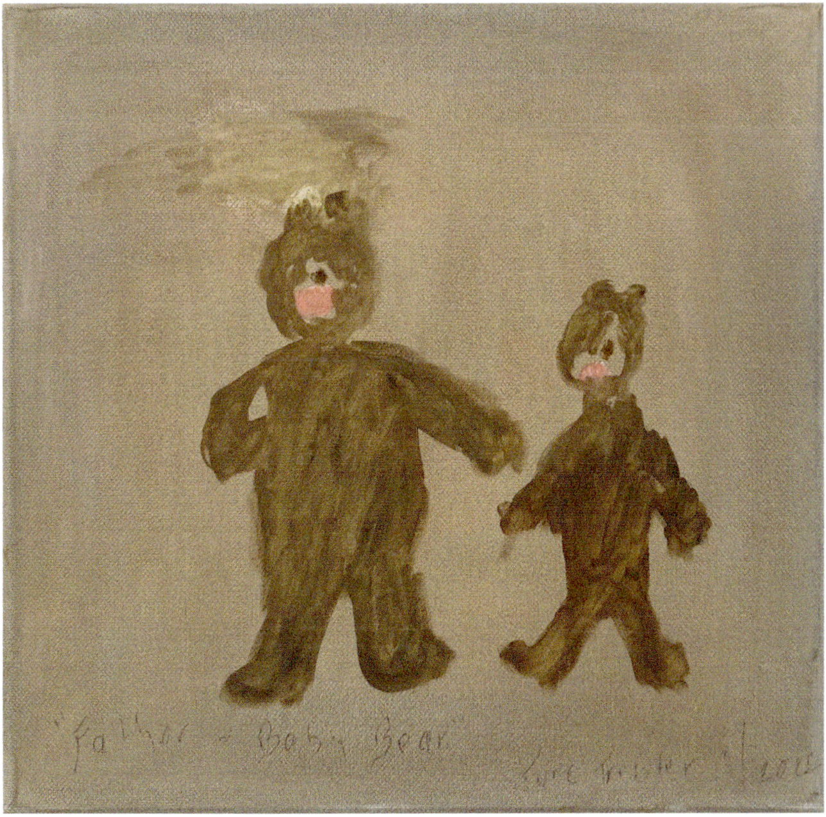

Father and Baby Bear Oil on canvas 30 x 30 cm August 2022

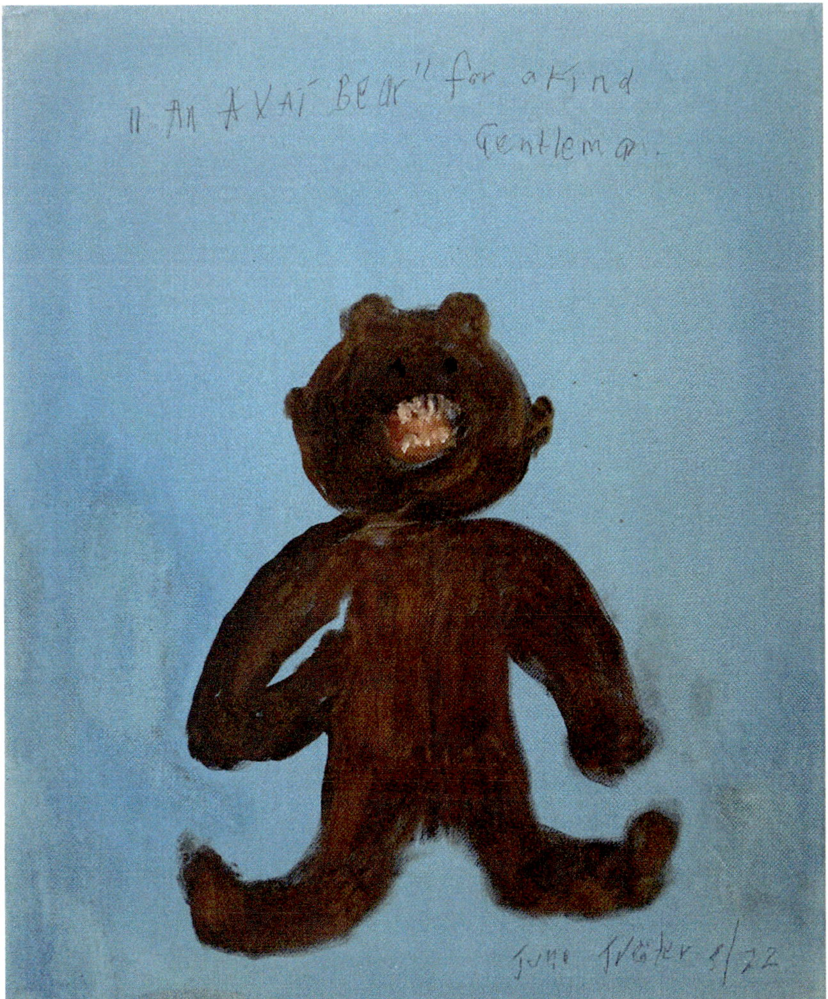

An Axat Bear 1 Oil on canvas 41 x 33 cm August 2022
Collection Sean Ashmore

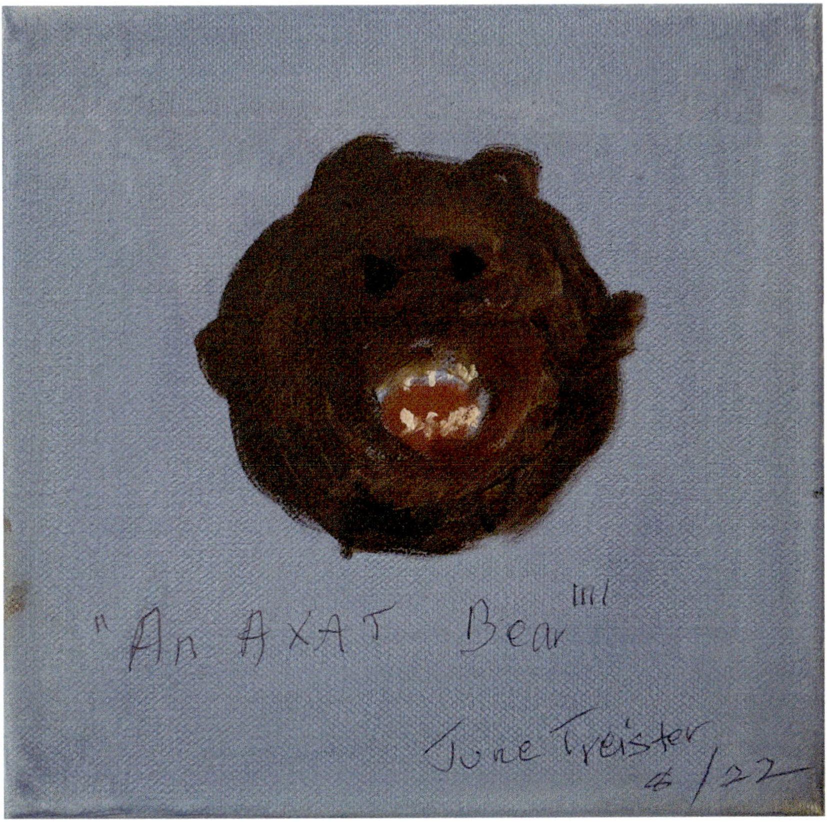

An Axat Bear 2 Oil on canvas 20 x 20 cm August 2022

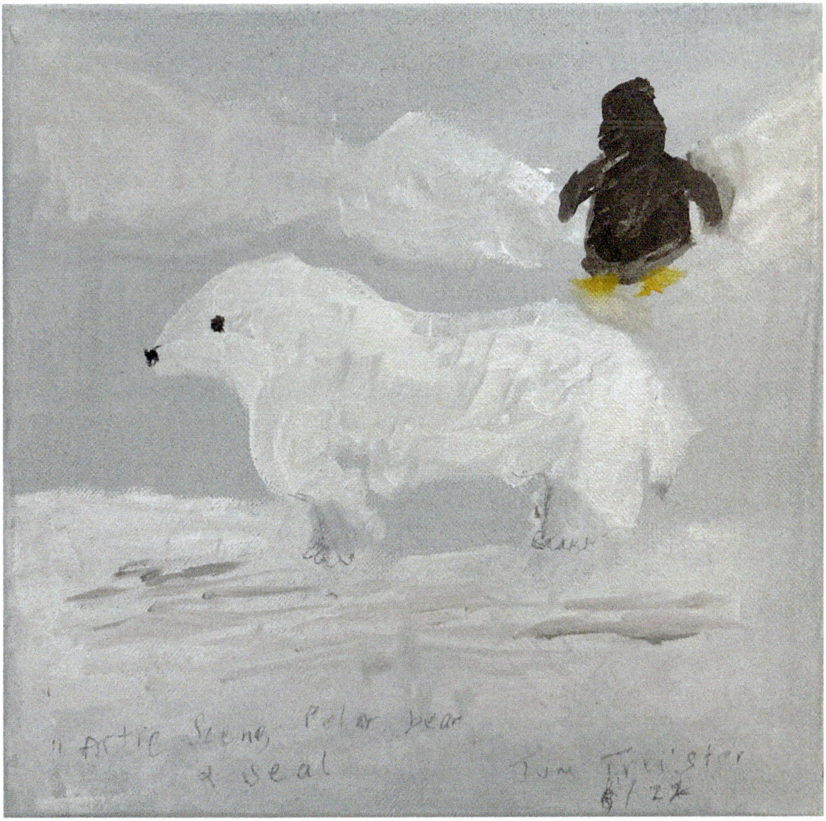

Arctic Scene, Polar bear and Seal Oil on canvas 30 x 30 cm August 2022

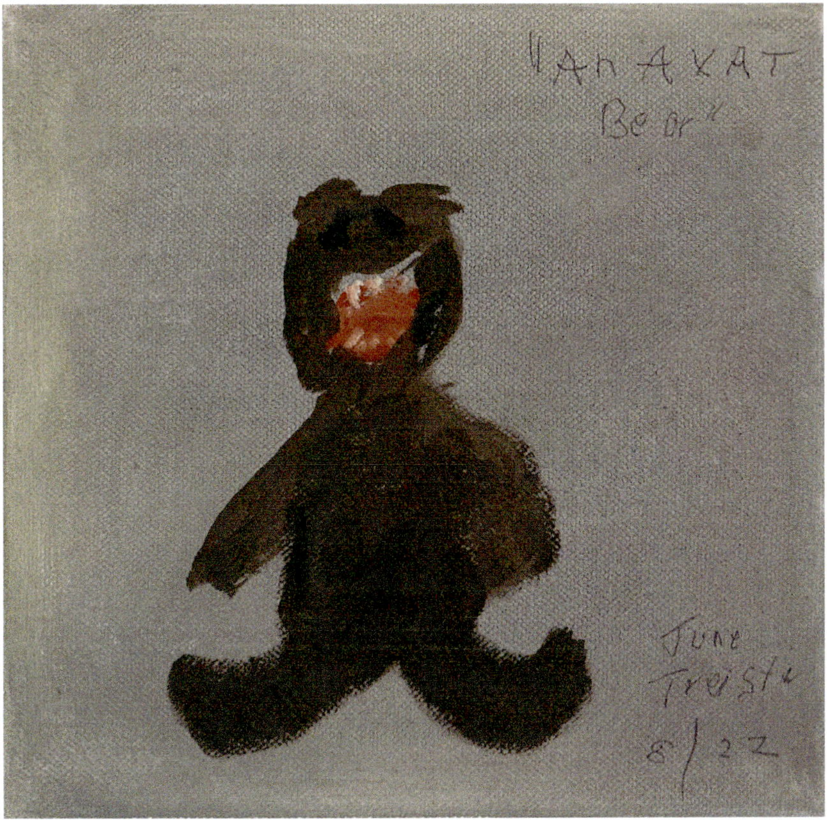

Axat Bear 3 Oil on canvas 20 x 20 cm August 2022

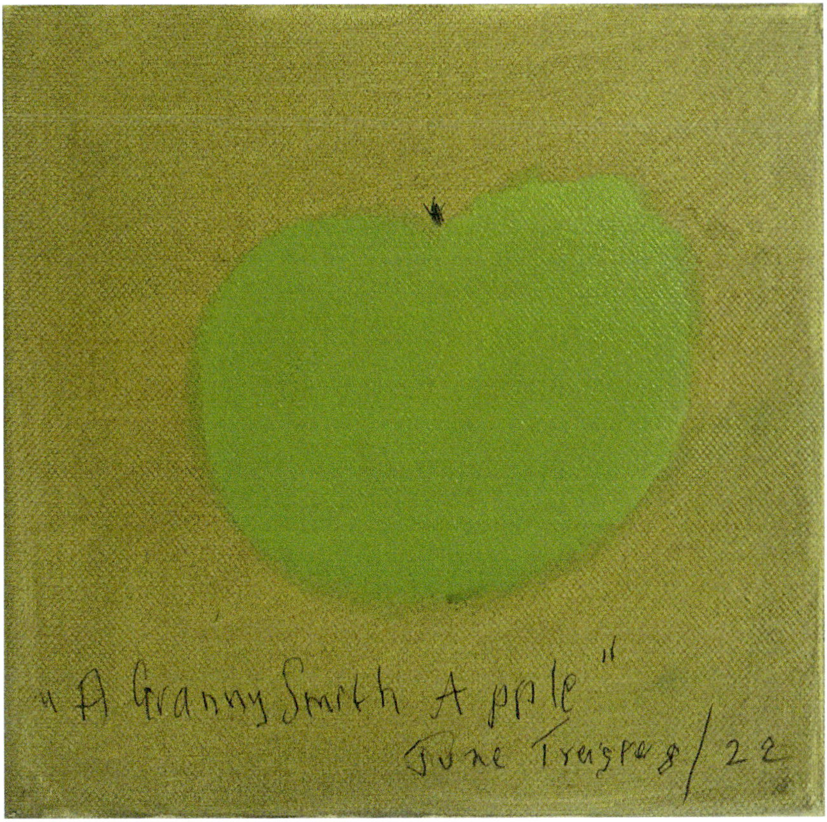

Granny Smith Apple Oil on canvas 20 x 20 cm August 2022

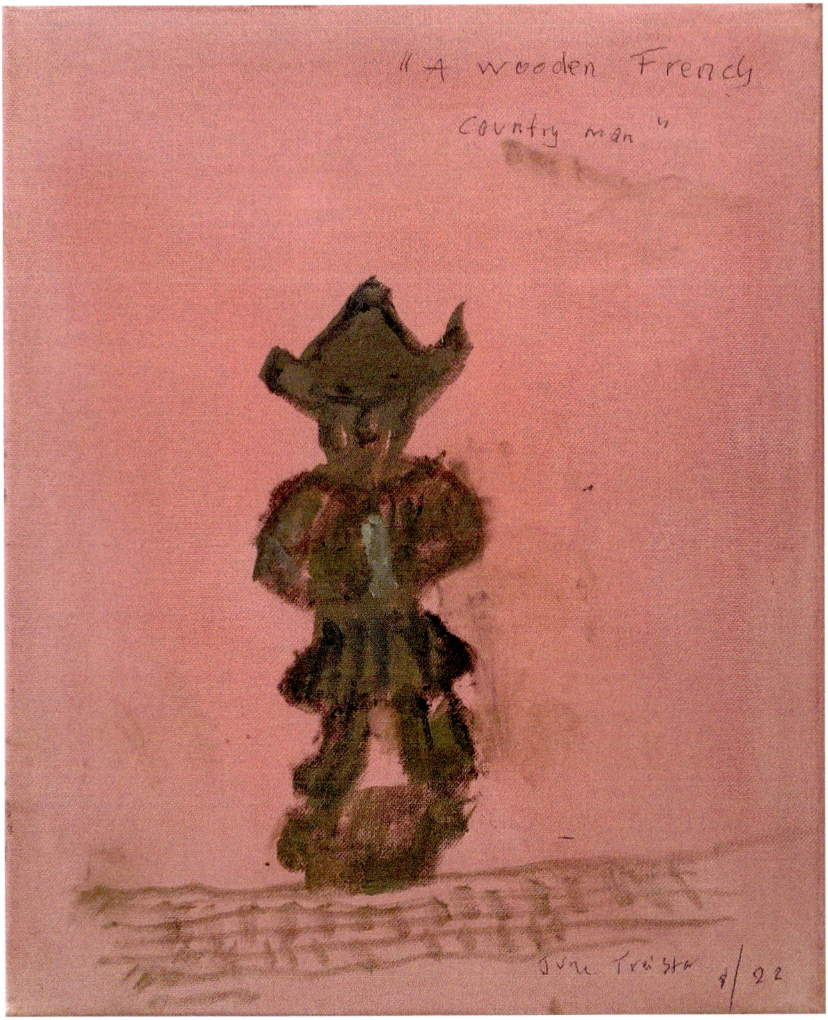

A Wooden French Country Man Oil on canvas 41 x 33 cm August 2022

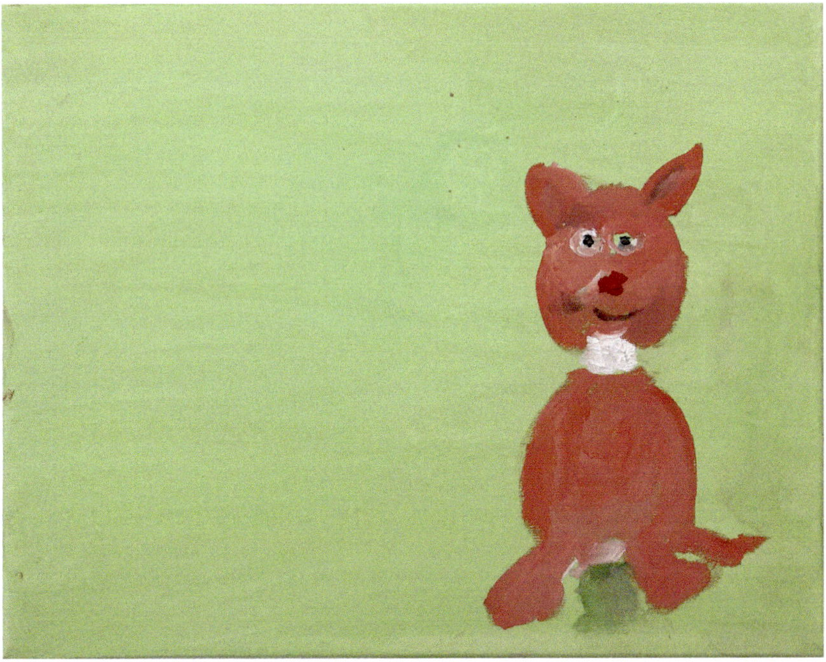

Pink Cat Oil on canvas 33 x 41 cm August 2022

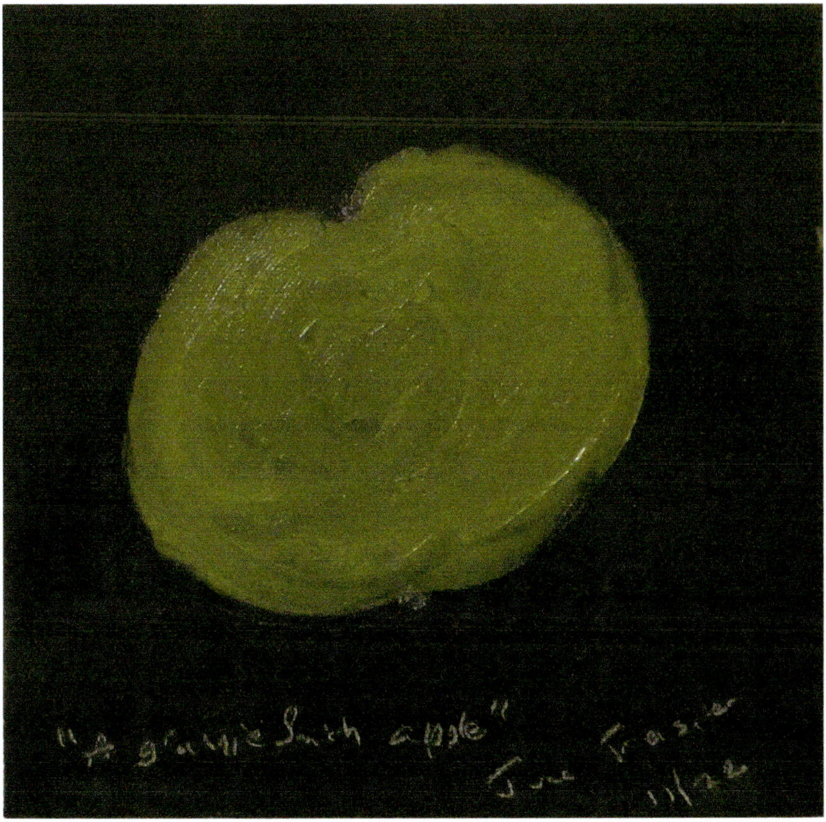

Granny Smith Apple with Dark Green Background Oil on canvas 20 x 20 cm 2022

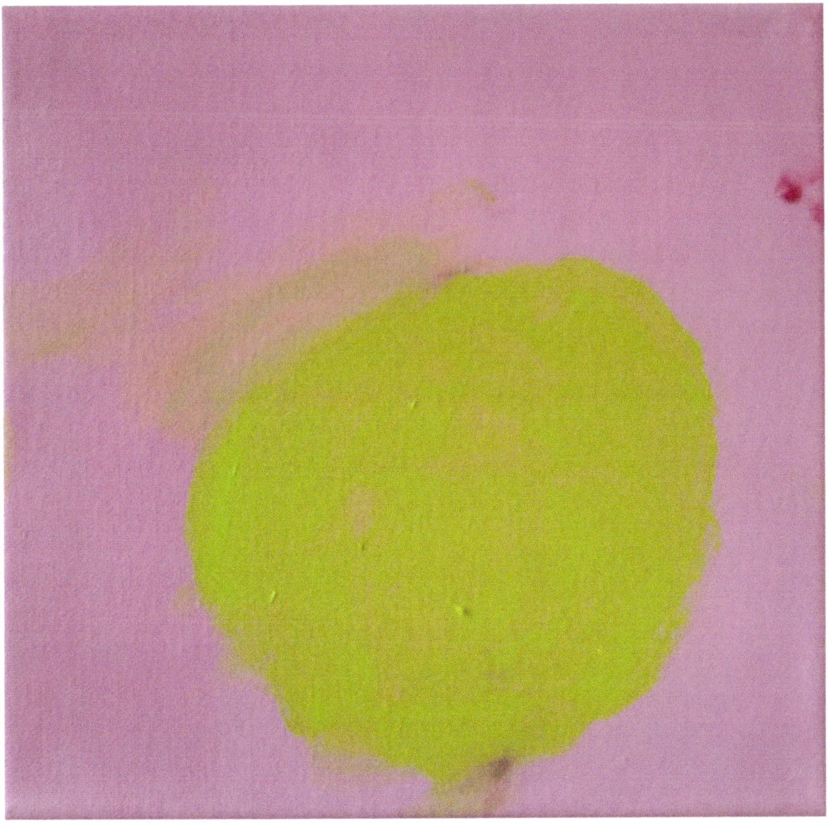

Granny Smith Apple with Pink Background Oil on canvas 20 x 20 cm 2023

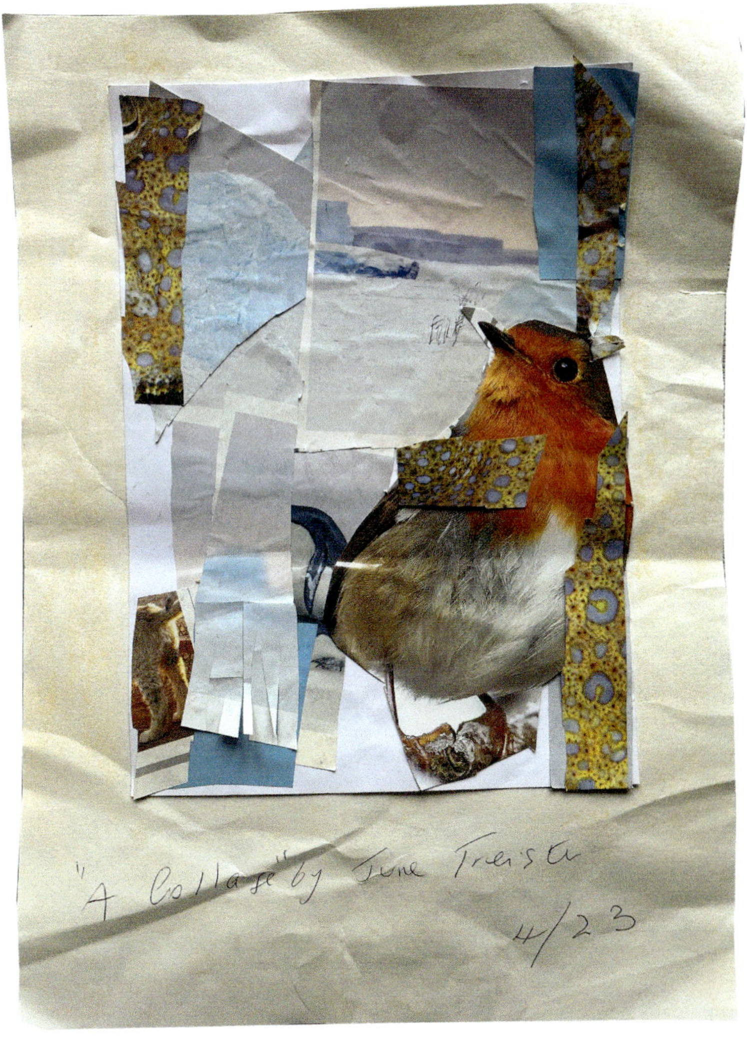

Robin Collage 42 x 29.7 cm April 2023

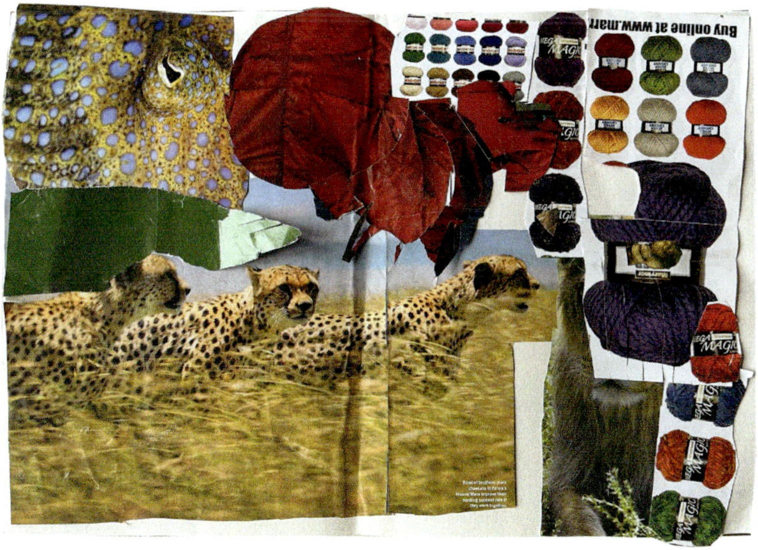

Tigers Collage 29.7 x 42 cm April 2023

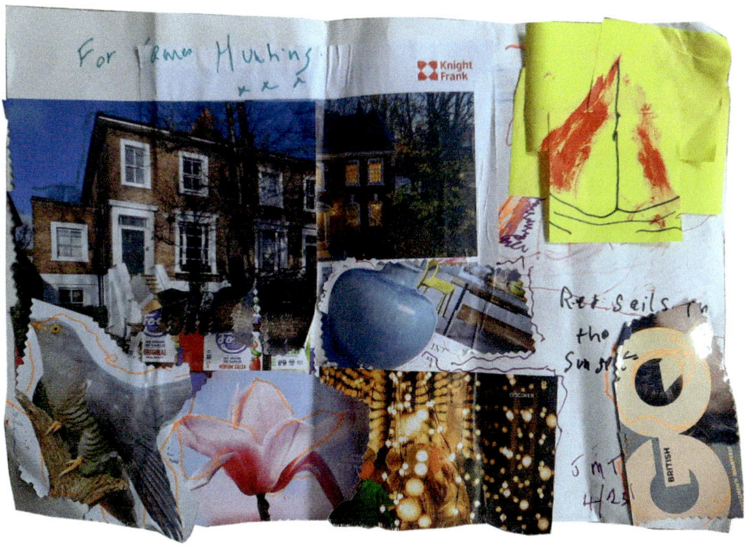

Red Sails in the Sunset Collage 29.7 x 42 cm April 2023

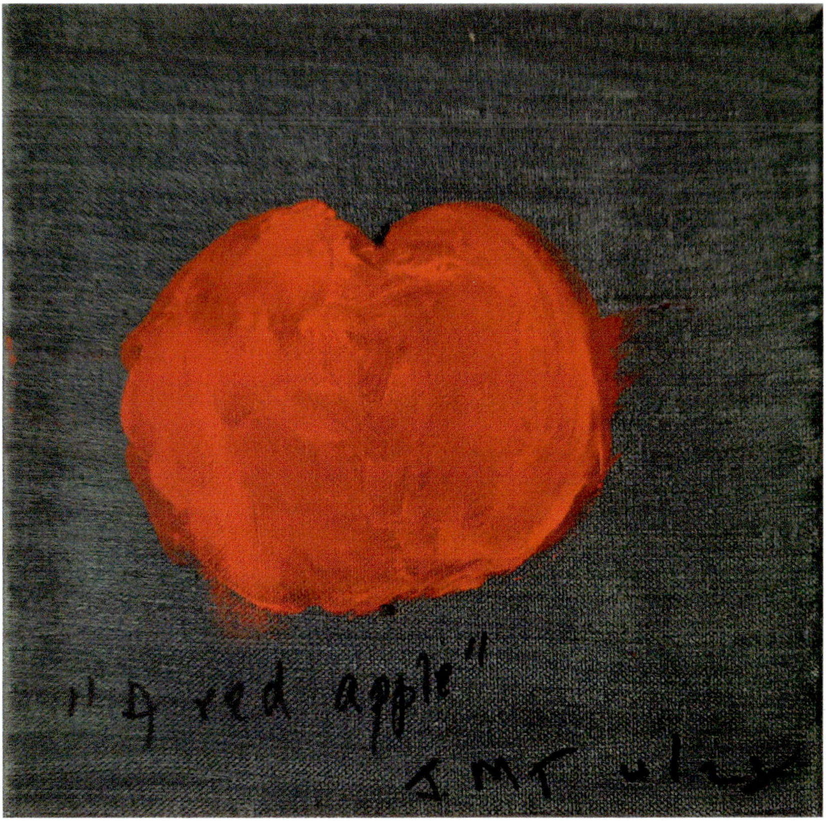

A Red Apple Oil on canvas 20 x 20 cm April 2023
Collection Adrian Dannatt

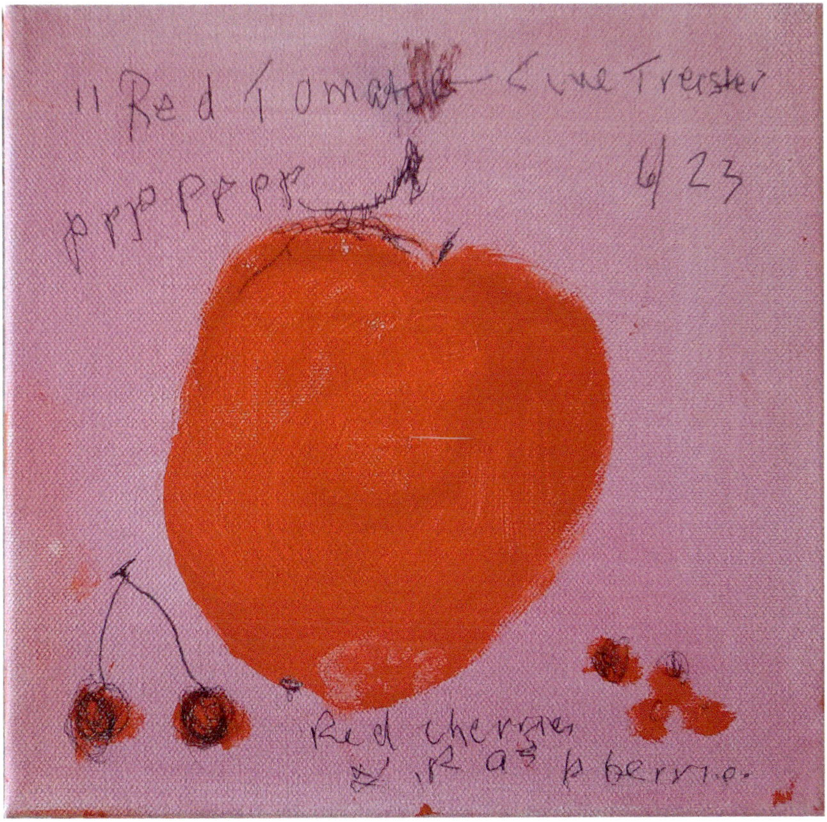

Red Tomato, Red Cherries and Raspberries Oil on canvas 20 x 20 cm June 2023

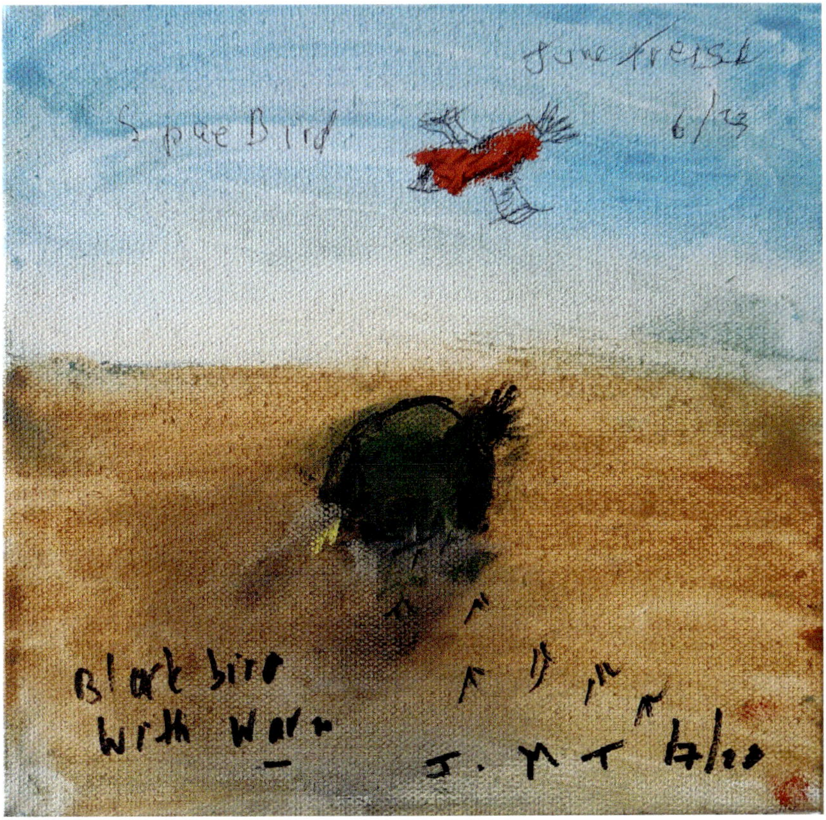

Space Bird with Worm Oil on canvas 20 x 20 cm July 2023

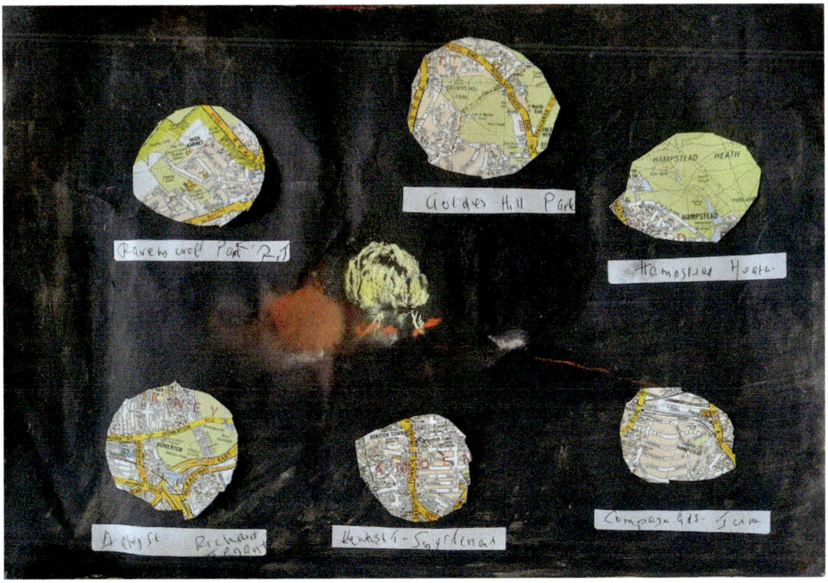

London Maps in Space Collage 29.7 x 42 cm July 2023

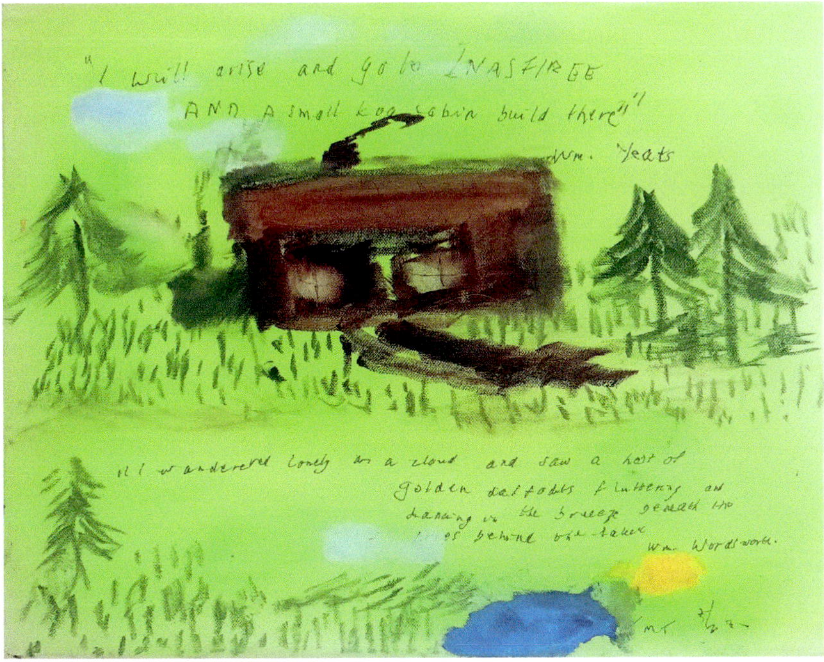

Yeats and Wordsworth Oil on canvas 33 x 41 cm July 2023

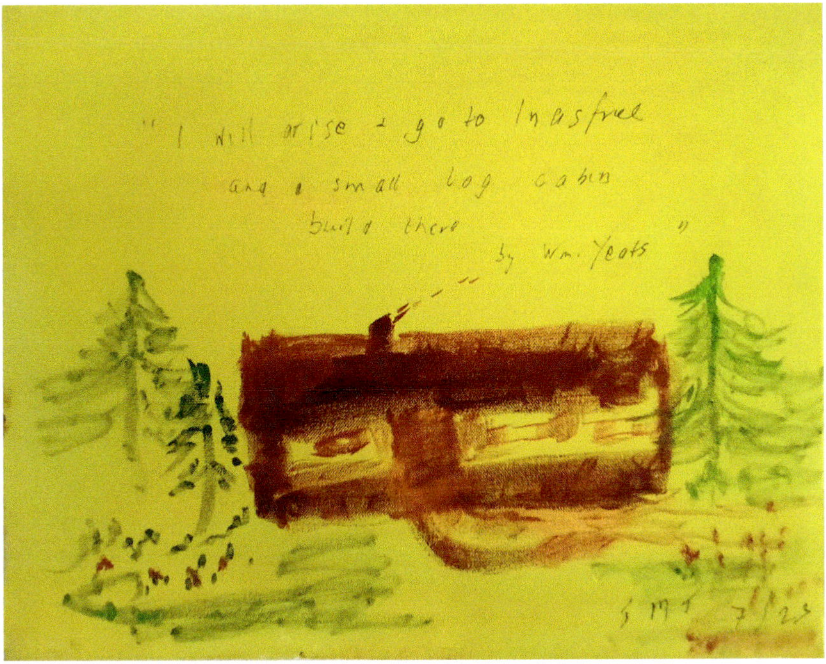

Yeats Oil on canvas 33 x 41 cm July 2023

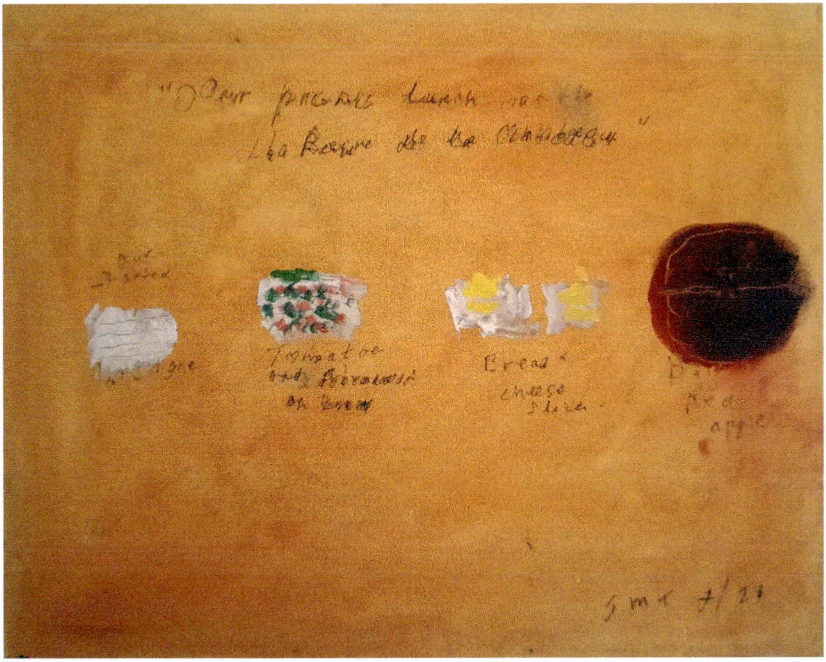

Picnic at Rennes le Chateau Oil on canvas 33 x 41 cm July 2023

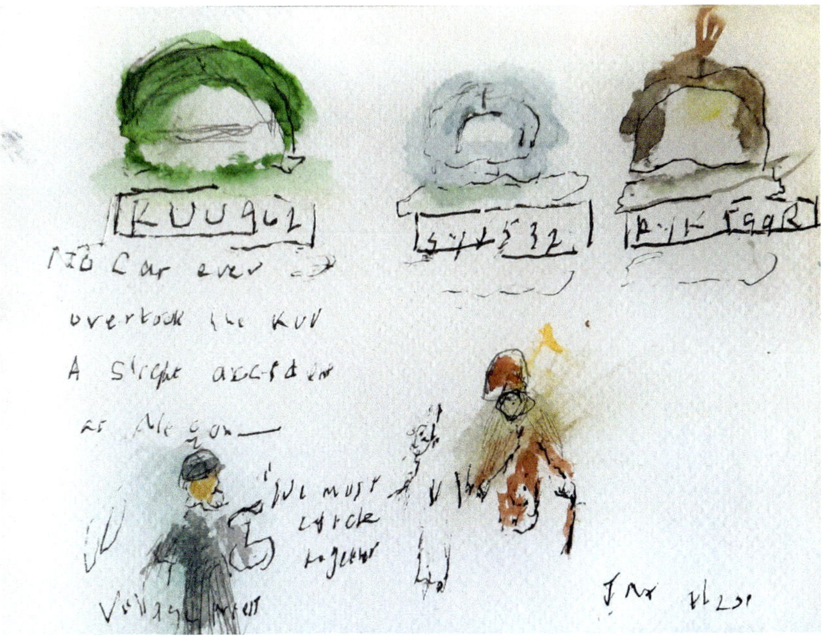

A History of My Car Number Plates + Accident Watercolour and pen on paper 15 x 21 cm July 2023

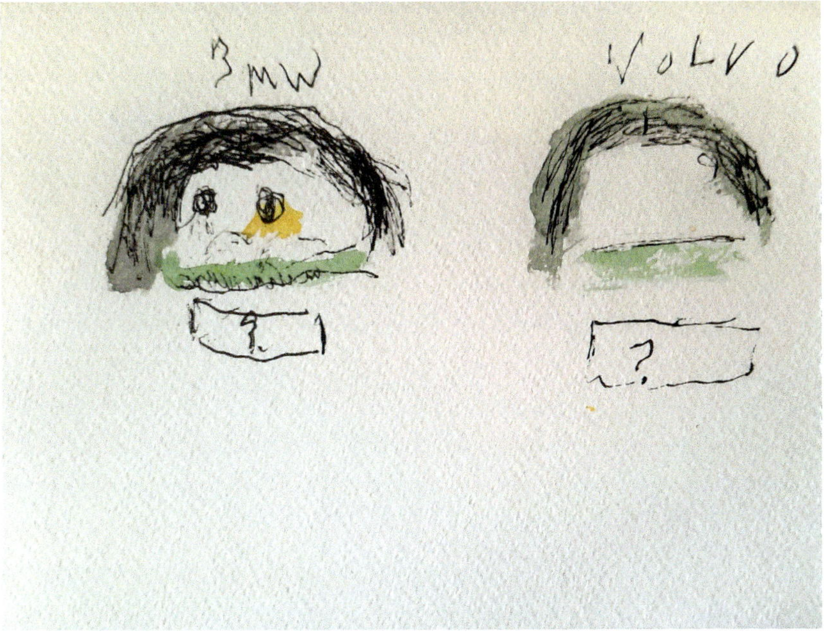

A History of My Car Number Plates 2 Watercolour and pen on paper 15 x 21 cm July 2023

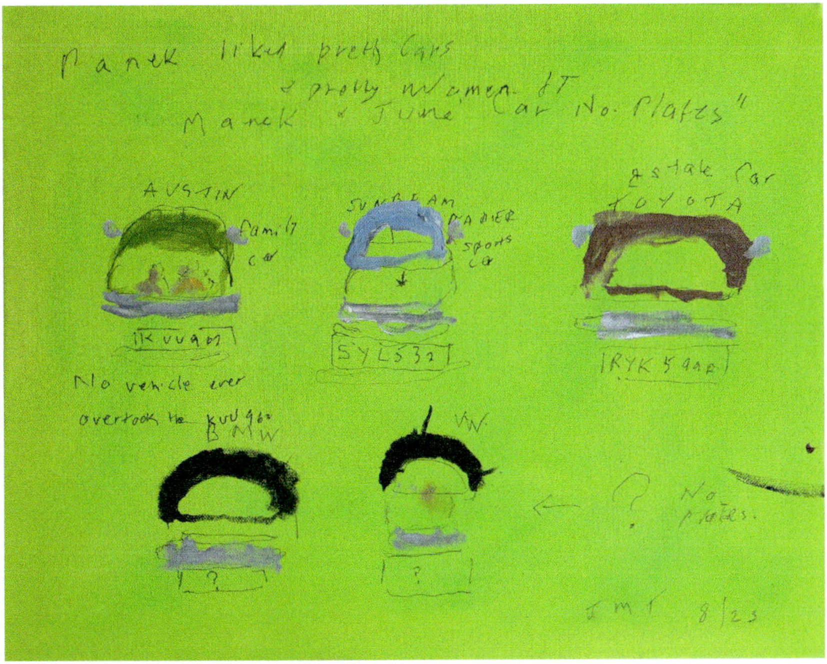

A History of My Car Number Plates Oil on canvas 33 x 41 cm July 2023

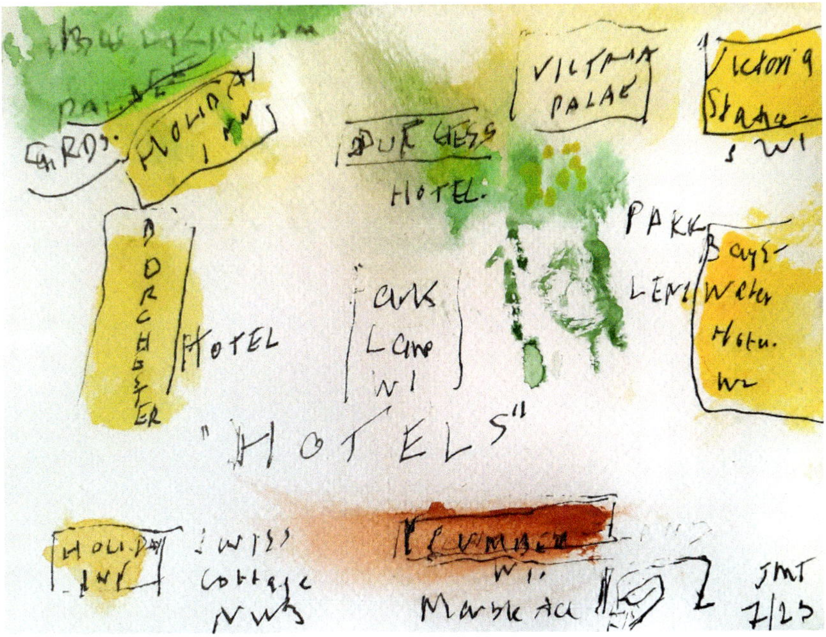

Hotels Watercolour and pen on paper 15 x 21 cm July 2023

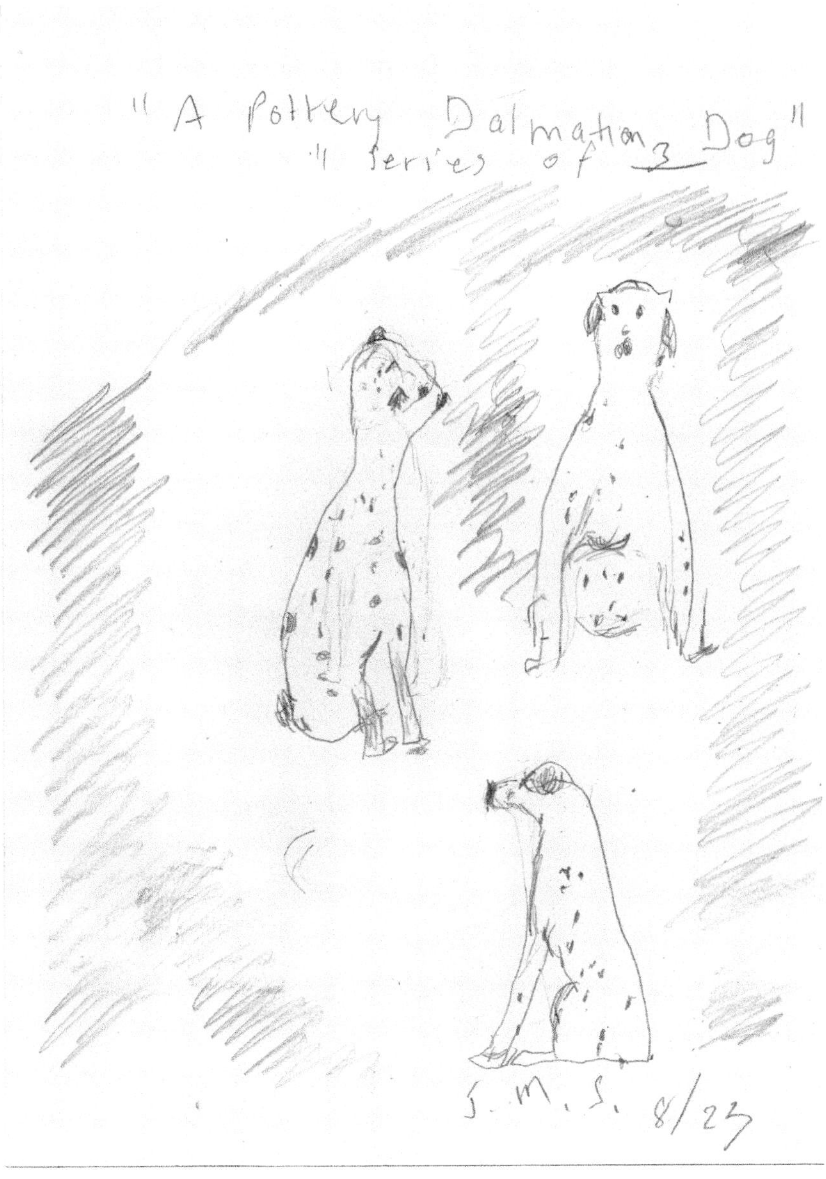

A Pottery Dalmation Dog (series of 3) Pencil on paper 29.7 x 21 cm August 2023
Collection Adrian Dannatt

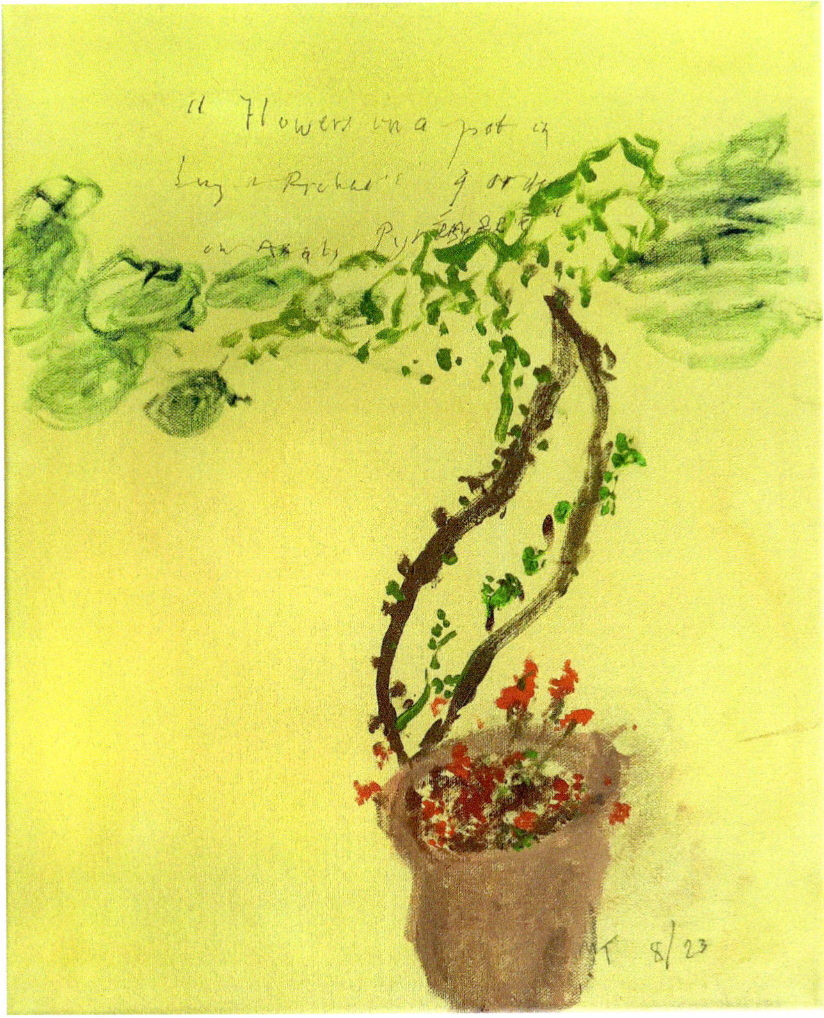

Flowerpot in the Pyrenees Oil on canvas 41 x 33 cm July 2023

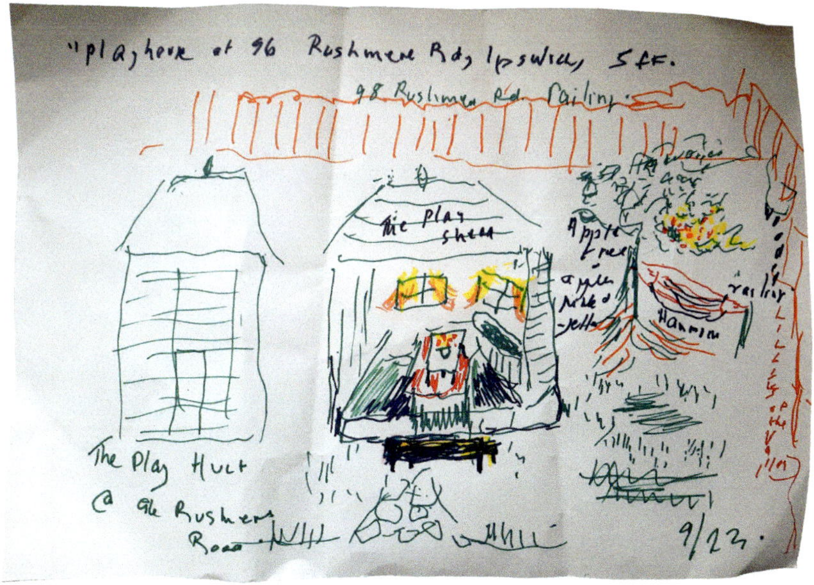

Play House Shed Hut Watercolour and pen on paper 15 x 21 cm September 2023

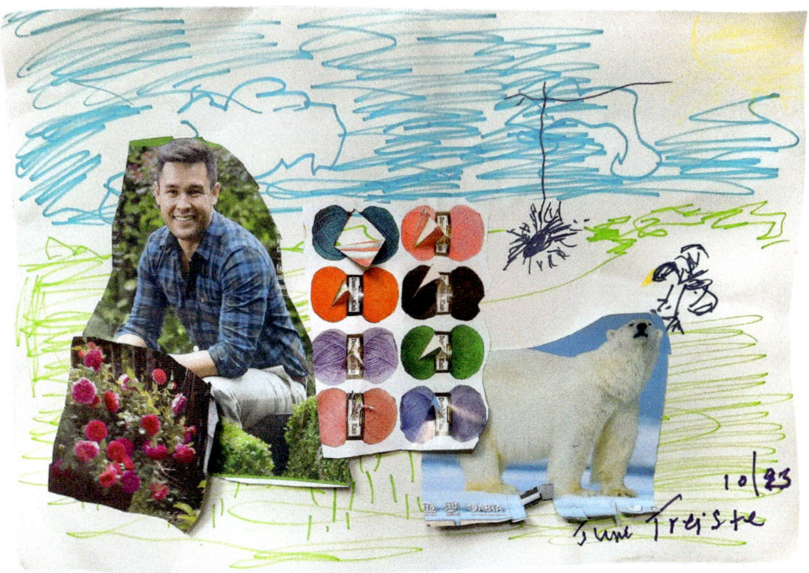

Polar Bear Collage 29.7 x 42 cm October 2023

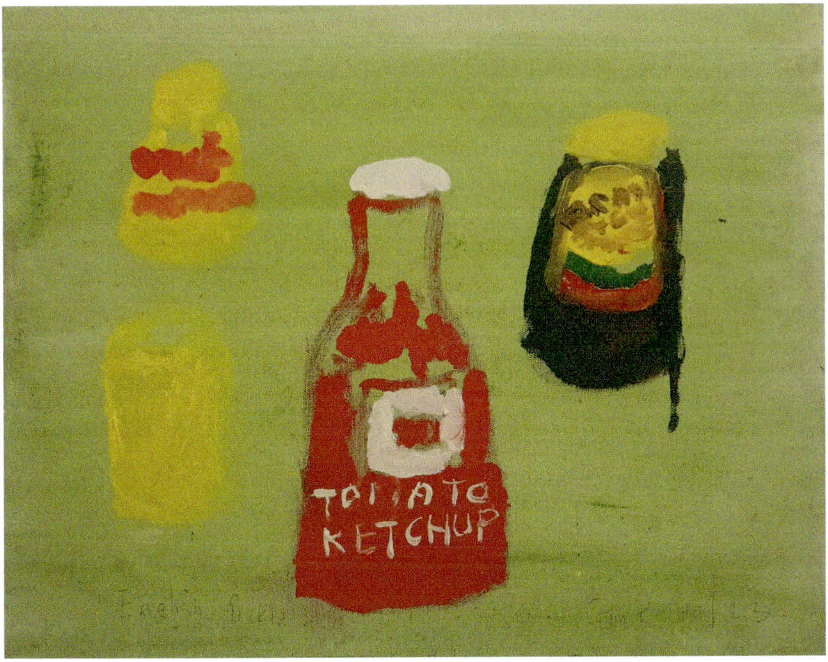

English Pickles: Colmans, Ketchup, Branston Oil on canvas 30 x 40 cm November 2023

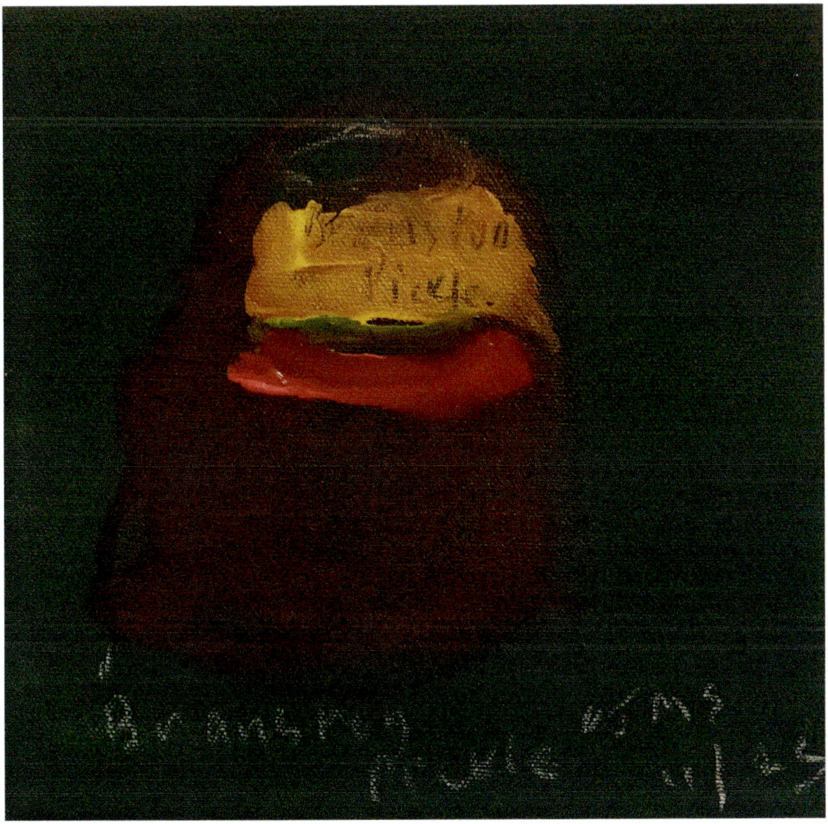

English Pickles: Branston Oil on canvas 20 x 20 cm November 2023

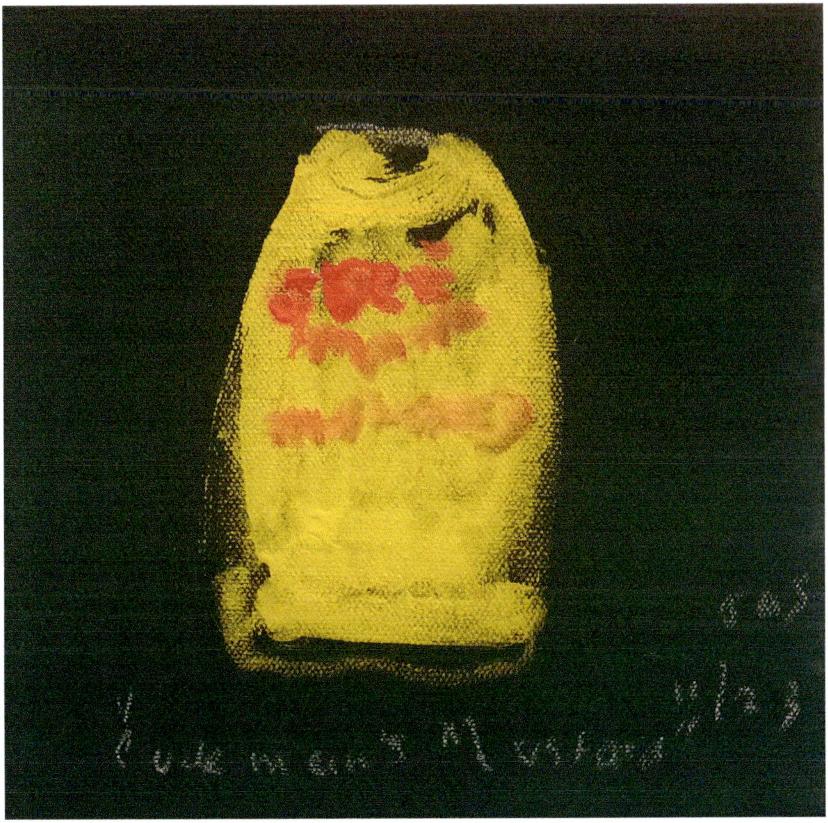

English Pickles: Colmans Oil on canvas 20 x 20 cm November 2023